Home Selling Secrets Unveiled

An Insider's Blueprint to Selling Your Home for Maximum Profits

TOI HOLLIDAY

Home Selling Secrets Unveiled

Home Selling Secrets Unveiled

Cover design by Bjou Brzee Creations.
Printed in the United States of America
First Printing: September 2023

Home Selling Secrets Unveiled

TABLE OF CONTENTS

CHAPTER 1

Introduction

In real estate, success is not a chance occurrence; it's the result of insightful, executable, and strategic planning with a deep understanding of the dynamics at play. "Home Selling Secrets Unveiled, an Insider's Blueprint to Selling Your Home for Maximum Profits" is more than a book—it's your compass, confidant, and key to unveiling the strategies that can make your home selling journey successful and extraordinary.

Within these pages, you will journey into self-discovery, learning how to harness your motivations, streamline your efforts, and embrace the power of detachment to maximize the sale of your home. We will walk through the meticulous steps of presenting your home at its best, curating spaces that captivate buyers and invoke the art of imagination.

Navigating professional services, from inspections to appraisals and expert repairs, will become a seamless part of your journey, ensuring your home stands ready for its spotlight moment. But it's not just about the physical—it's about your mindset, purpose, and ability to navigate the intricate details of negotiations.

Each chapter is a revelation—a guiding light that empowers you to avoid common pitfalls, harness the agent advantage, and apply the art of strategic pricing like a maestro. By the time you reach the final pages, you'll have uncovered a treasure trove of insights, techniques, and secrets that are tailor-made to elevate your home selling experience.

This book isn't just about selling a property; it's about crafting a narrative, about shaping the story of your home's next chapter. It's about realizing that your home isn't just a structure—it's a canvas upon which dreams are painted, and those dreams continue even after the keys change hands.

So, embrace this book as your partner, mentor, and guide, whether you're downsizing, upsizing, relocating, or launching into a new life chapter. Together, we'll navigate the intricate tapestry of home selling, uncovering the hidden gems that can turn your journey into a symphony of success.

The path is set, and the blueprint is yours—let's begin this journey together.

CHAPTER 2

Cracking the Home Selling Code: Unveiling Insider Strategies

Imagine yourself at the threshold of a remarkable journey—one that goes beyond the ordinary bounds of home selling. In this chapter, we embark on an exploration of the secrets and strategies that transform a routine property transaction into a symphony of success. Welcome to the world of insider mastery, where the art of home selling is elevated to an extraordinary level.

The Game-Changing Insight: Beneath the Surface

As you stand on the brink of your home selling adventure, it's essential to understand that this is not a mere transaction—it's an opportunity to transform your property into a masterpiece. The journey begins with the revelation that successful home selling is not just about putting your property on the market; it's about discerning the hidden nuances, recognizing market trends, and unveiling the insights that insiders hold dear.

Strategic Proficiency: Beyond Expectations

Prepare to transcend the confines of conventional approaches. Insider strategies are the key to unlocking exceptional results. They allow you to maneuver the currents of the real estate market with a finesse that goes beyond what is expected. These strategies are your compass, guiding you toward the realm of positioning your property as a work of art that stands apart from the crowd.

Crafting Your Unique Selling Proposition: An Artistry of Words

Picture your property not as a structure, but as a story waiting to be told. The art of home selling transcends brick and mortar—it's a narrative woven with the threads of potential, emotion, and aspiration. Insider strategies reveal how to infuse your property with character and meaning, creating a unique selling proposition that resonates deeply with prospective buyers.

Tailoring for Success: The Elegance of Personalization

Every property has a distinct personality, a unique essence that can be enhanced with precision. Whether your property is a cozy haven, a sprawling estate, or anything in between, insiders recognize the importance of customization. Discover the power of tailoring your presentation to match the dreams and desires of your target audience, leaving an indelible mark on their imaginations.

Navigating the Currents of the Market: A Virtuoso's Insight

In the realm of insider strategies, the market is not an enigma—it's an orchestration of trends and fluctuations waiting to be conducted. By immersing yourself in the art of market analysis, you gain the power to set your listing price with finesse and time your entry for maximum impact. Embrace the role of a virtuoso, navigating the market's currents with confidence.

From Listing to Closing: Orchestrating Success

The journey from listing to closing is not a disjointed collection of tasks; it's a harmonious symphony conducted by the maestro of insider strategies. With each step, you'll wield the baton of intent, ensuring that every action resonates with purpose. Insider strategies transform your journey into an artful procession—a procession that culminates in the final crescendo of a successful sale.

Your Path to Mastery: The Overture

As you journey through these pages, keep in mind that you're not just absorbing knowledge; you're immersing yourself in the art of mastery. Let this chapter be your overture—a prelude to the symphony of insights that awaits. By the final note, you'll stand equipped with the tools to navigate the complexities of the market, the strategies to position your property with finesse, and the confidence to achieve unparalleled success.

Prepare to venture beyond the ordinary and embrace the extraordinary. The stage is set, the curtain rises, and you are the star of this performance. With each word you read, you're drawing back the curtain on a realm of possibility—a realm where insider strategies unlock the doors to the pinnacle of home selling achievement.

CHAPTER 3

Seller Mindset:
Know Your Purpose and Stay Focused

As you start selling your home, the foundation of your success lies in the strategic steps you take and the depths of your intentions and mindset. Imagine your intentions as the compass guiding your decisions and your mindset as the driving force propelling you toward your goal. In this chapter, we uncover the transformative effects of empowered intentions and a positive mindset in the realm of home selling.

Understanding the Power of Purpose

Your decision to sell your home results from many factors, each carrying its weight and significance. Whether you're seeking more space for a growing family, downsizing for simplicity, or making a strategic financial move, your purpose shapes the trajectory of your selling journey. This purpose is the compass that guides your actions, imbuing them with intention and direction.

Delve deep into your motivations—explore the desires and goals driving your decision. Begin by creating a quiet space for introspection, away from the clamor of daily life. Sit down with a notepad and pen, inviting your thoughts to flow freely. Consider the reasons that led you to decide to sell your home. Is it about creating a better environment for your loved ones, seizing a new opportunity, or embarking on a fresh chapter of life? These are the cornerstones of your purpose, waiting to be unveiled.

As you engage in this journey of self-discovery, go beyond surface-level explanations. Uncover the emotions intertwined with your motivations. Are you seeking comfort, security, adventure, or the thrill of embracing change? Each layer you peel back brings you closer to the core of your purpose.

Your purpose isn't confined to practical considerations alone. Envision the life you aspire to after the sale—a life filled with contentment, fulfillment, and new horizons. Imagine the emotions that will accompany your achievement. Will the move bring a sense of relief, excitement, or the satisfaction of realizing a long-held dream? Let these emotions guide your exploration.

Involve your loved ones in this introspective journey. Initiate open conversations with family members to gather their insights and feelings. Their perspectives can offer valuable insights into the collective purpose behind the decision. Consider how the sale aligns with shared dreams and aspirations, further illuminating the depth of your purpose.

Additionally, ponder the financial and strategic implications of the sale. Are you seeking to leverage your property's equity for future investments or long-term financial security? Clarify how your purpose aligns with your broader goals, both personal and financial.

As you navigate this process of self-discovery, remember that your purpose is uniquely yours. It's the driving force infusing every action with intention, ensuring each decision aligns with your more excellent vision. Write down your reflections, capturing the essence of your purpose in words. This written declaration will serve as a guiding light, reminding you of the "why" behind your actions when challenges arise.

Identifying your purpose isn't just an exercise—it's the cornerstone of your empowered selling journey. With your purpose as your compass, you'll find that every step becomes infused with intention, every decision resonates with meaning, and every achievement aligns with a more excellent vision. As you move forward, carry your purpose with you, let it shape your interactions, and allow it to empower you to make the most of this transformative experience.

Guiding Your Emotional Journey

When selling your home due to significant life events such as divorce, loss of a loved one, or career shifts, the process goes beyond the physical transaction. It becomes a deeply emotional journey that demands your attention and understanding. Your decision is intricately woven into the fabric of your experiences, memories, and aspirations. From the exhilaration of embracing new opportunities to the poignant sense of bidding farewell to familiar spaces, these emotions are valid and essential to acknowledge.

Amidst these emotional currents, it's vital to remain centered and focused. Life events can shake the very foundation of your emotional and mental equilibrium, making it even more crucial to navigate this process mindfully. By recognizing and accepting the emotions that arise, you create space for grace and perspective. Rather than being overwhelmed by feelings, you can harness them as catalysts for growth and transformation.

Redirecting Your Energy

In times of change and transition, emotions can be both a source of strength and a potential challenge. To ensure a successful home selling journey, consider channeling these emotions as a driving force for your purpose. Let your feelings become the compass that guides your actions and decisions. For instance, the memory-laden rooms of your home can be transformed into a canvas of possibility, where you can paint new beginnings and envision the next chapter of your life.

Staying focused on your goals is paramount. It's natural for emotions to ebb and flow, but by grounding yourself in your purpose, you can navigate this intricate process with resilience. Remember, every decision you make, every step you take, is an opportunity to honor your journey and shape your future. Your home selling experience, amid life's twists and turns, becomes a testament to your strength and the vision you hold for what lies ahead.

Nurturing Clear Intentions

After delving into the heart of your purpose, the next step is to nurture those intentions into focused clarity. Imagine your intentions as a well-crafted map, designed to navigate you through the intricate path that unfolds as you sell your home. In this journey, every decision is a pivotal crossroad, and every choice becomes an opportunity to honor the purpose you've set.

Visualize your intentions as the lighthouse that illuminates your way through the often complex decisions ahead. If your aim is to upsize your living space to accommodate a growing family, your intentions could take the form of an envisioned haven where cherished moments and togetherness flourish. Picture the rooms that will echo with laughter, the spaces where stories will be shared, and the foundation for future memories.

Conversely, if downsizing for a simpler life is your objective, your intentions might manifest as a vision of tranquility and freedom from clutter. Envision the serenity of minimalism, where every item serves a purpose and where the space around you breathes with ease. Picture the joy of unburdened living and the ability to focus on what truly matters.

Guiding Your Decisions

With your intentions firmly in place, the decisions you make throughout the home selling process take on new significance. Each step, whether it's preparing your property for listing, considering offers, or negotiating terms, is a chance to align with the purpose you've set. Your intentions serve as the compass that keeps you on course, even when the waters of change become uncertain.

Let your intentions influence the trajectory of your decisions. When faced with choices, reflect on whether they resonate with the purpose you've embraced. Ask yourself if a particular option brings you closer to the ideal space you've envisioned. By doing so, you create a consistent thread that ties your actions to your aspirations, providing a sense of direction and purpose.

Steering Toward Fulfillment

Just as a rudder guides a ship toward its desired destination, your intentions act as the guiding force in your home selling journey. They give you a sense of purpose, allowing you to navigate the complexities of the process with clarity and determination. With each step you take in line with your intentions, you are moving closer to your desired port—the realization of your goals, aspirations, and the future you've envisioned.

Forging a Positive Mindset

Within the realm of selling your home, your mindset assumes the role of an artist shaping your entire experience. The power of a positive mindset extends beyond your emotional state, permeating every interaction with potential buyers and your approach to surmounting challenges. Embrace an attitude brimming with possibilities, where each showing, and negotiation becomes a purposeful stride toward realizing your desired outcome. Let go of doubt, as negativity only acts as an impediment to your progress. Envision your success vividly, nurturing an optimistic presence that resonates warmly with those you engage. In the face of obstacles, remember that setbacks are but the steppingstones leading to transformative breakthroughs.

Anchoring in Resilience

The journey of selling a home isn't devoid of challenges—unexpected twists may test your patience. However, armed with empowered intentions and a positive mindset, you possess the capacity to navigate these challenges with resilience. Embrace setbacks as an opportunity for growth and learning. Shift your perspective to see obstacles as moments of transformation and setbacks as the catalysts that propel you closer to your goal.

Questions to Reflect Upon:

1. Why Are You Selling Your Home?
   - What's driving your decision to sell?
   - Are there specific goals or outcomes you're aiming for with this sale?

2. How Will Selling Your Home Impact Your Life?
   - How does this home sale align with your future plans?
   - Will it enhance your life in some meaningful way?

A written declaration of your purpose will serve as a guiding light, providing clarity and motivation, especially when you encounter challenges along the way.

CHAPTER 4

Detaching with Purpose: Managing Emotional Attachment to Maximize Sales

Selling a home is similar to conducting a symphony of emotions—a harmonious blend of cherished memories, monumental milestones, and the profound sense of place that has lovingly nurtured your life. Your home stands as a living testament to countless chapters in your journey—a repository of laughter, tears, and the numerous little moments that have woven the fabric of your existence. As you stand on the threshold of selling, a juncture marked by nostalgia and anticipation, you find yourself at the crossroads of heart and strategy. It is precisely at this crossroads that the need for detachment becomes both apparent and imperative. Welcome to a chapter that delves into the intricate art of detaching with purpose—an art that empowers you to navigate the delicate interplay between sentiment and strategy with grace and wisdom.

Imagine your home as a sanctuary of memories—an embodiment of laughter shared with family, quiet contemplation in cozy corners, and the vibrant celebrations that have echoed within its walls. This sanctuary has been a steadfast companion throughout the tapestry of your life, a canvas upon which the vibrant strokes of your story have been painted. Yet, as you embark on the journey to sell, a nuanced truth emerges—the transition from homeowner to seller entails a transformative shift in perspective. This shift unveils the artistry of detachment—a means of transitioning the sanctuary of memories into an inviting canvas primed for the creation of new stories.

With each room you step into, the walls whisper echoes of experiences, and each corner harbors the essence of emotions once lived. These spaces where you've created unforgettable memories are filled with the fabric of your identity, and the decision to sell isn't a mere transaction—it's an emotional crossroads. Within this emotional juncture lies an invitation to embrace the purpose of detachment—a purpose that guides you toward an empowered transition.

To detach with purpose is to honor the significance of your home's history while making space for the potential of its future. It's a process that invites you to gaze at your home through a new lens, transforming it from a vessel of personal experiences to a canvas upon which stories of new families will be painted. With each treasured memory you detach from, you're creating room for fresh stories to unfold, for the laughter of new occupants to fill the rooms, and for the tapestry of life to continue evolving.

As you navigate this journey, envision your home as an anthology—a collection of stories that have shaped your life's narrative. By detaching with purpose, you're not bidding farewell to these stories; instead, you're curating the stage for new tales to unfold. Your home, once a vessel of your experiences, now becomes a vessel of potential—a platform for others to script their own chapters.

Detaching with purpose isn't about severing emotional ties; it's about transmuting them into a gift of opportunity, growth, and transformation. It's about stepping into the role of steward, where your cherished memories become the foundation upon which new dreams are built. As you embark on this journey of purposeful detachment, remember that every room you declutter, every memory you gracefully release, paves the way for a new chapter—both for you and the fortunate soul who will call your property home.

Prepare to navigate the emotional currents of home selling with intention and grace. The art of detaching with purpose is honoring the past, celebrating the present, and embracing the future—a journey that empowers you to release with love, detach with purpose, and transition with grace.

The Dance of Attachment and Detachment

Your home is more than walls and rooms; it's a vessel of experiences that resonate deeply with your life's journey. From the laughter that echoed in the halls to the quiet moments of solitude, every corner holds a piece of your story. Recognizing this emotional tapestry is the first step toward a purposeful detachment. Understand that while these memories are precious, they don't define the future path of your property.

The Vision of a Blank Canvas

Imagine your home as a blank canvas—a canvas that holds the potential to become someone else's masterpiece. As you detach, envision your home as a canvas where new stories take shape and fresh memories come to life. Embrace the notion that the next owner will infuse the property with their dreams and aspirations, just as you did. This vision transforms the process of letting go into an act of passing the torch to the next chapter.

Prepare for Imagination

To effectively declutter with intent, adopt the approach of a seasoned organizer. Think of decluttering and depersonalizing as a chance to invite potential buyers to visualize themselves inhabiting the space. When you remove personal belongings, family photos, and keepsakes, you're not eliminating your presence; you're establishing an opportunity for potential buyers to envision their own narrative. By carefully shaping the environment, you create a platform for their aspirations to flourish.

Emotions in the Negotiation Arena

The negotiation phase can often stir the embers of attachment. Emotions may rise as offers are evaluated and counteroffers are made. In these moments, the purpose of detachment becomes a guiding light. Remind yourself that the negotiations are a step toward your goal of a successful sale. Approach each decision with clarity, drawing strength from the understanding that detaching doesn't diminish the significance of your memories. It's important to keep in mind that during negotiations, offers are not based on the memories you've made in your home. Instead, they are primarily rooted in what potential buyers perceive as the property's fair market value. Sentimental value, while deeply meaningful to you, doesn't directly influence the objective worth of your home in the real estate market. A buyer's perspective is based on a combination of factors, including the property's features, condition, and the memories they envision creating in their new home.

The Empowerment of Purposeful Detachment

Detaching with purpose doesn't mean severing emotional ties; it means channeling emotions into empowerment. As you transition, consider donating or repurposing items that hold sentimental value. Transforming these objects into gifts for others or art pieces can be a cathartic experience. Embrace the release, allowing it to pave the way for a new chapter of growth and discovery.

Cultivating a Mindset of Grace

As you navigate this path of detachment, grace should be your unwavering companion. Embrace the moments of nostalgia without allowing them to overshadow your primary goal. Greet potential buyers with the realization that they are on a quest to create their own story in a new place, just as you once did. Your capacity to gracefully lead them through the property signifies your intention to pass on the legacy while ushering in fresh beginnings.

Your Purposeful Transition

As you immerse yourself in the exploration of detaching with purpose, remember that this chapter isn't about severing ties—it's about transitioning with intention. It's about embracing the duality of sentiment and strategy. By honoring the memories while opening the door to new possibilities, you achieve the delicate balance that maximizes your property's appeal.

Prepare to embark on this purposeful transition with the wisdom of recognizing the value of emotional connection while remaining open to the transformative potential of change. Your journey to managing emotional attachment is not a farewell; it's an invitation for a new chapter to begin.

Questions to Reflect Upon:

1. How Do You Feel About the Idea of Parting with Your Home?
    - Explore your emotional response to the prospect of selling your home.
    - What sentiments or concerns come to mind when thinking about letting go?

2. What Benefits Do You Envision After the Sale?
    - Consider the positive outcomes that will follow once the sale is complete.
    - How will letting go emotionally contribute to achieving your goals?

Documenting your purpose in writing will act as a guiding beacon, providing clarity and motivation, especially when confronted with challenges along your path.

CHAPTER 5

Navigating Professional Services: Inspections, Appraisals, and Repairs

In this chapter, we'll delve into a trio of essential stages that hold the power to shape your trajectory toward a triumphant home sale: inspections, appraisals, and professional repairs. As you take your first steps into selling your home, view these expert services as trusted allies, offering you invaluable guidance and a newfound sense of empowerment.

For a moment, imagine that you're on a grand expedition into the uncharted territory of real estate. See yourself equipped with a simple compass and a comprehensive map that reveals the terrain ahead and points out potential pitfalls and hidden treasures. This is precisely what a preemptive home inspection provides—an in-depth and comprehensive examination of every detail and corner of your property.

Think of it as an adventure of discovery, where you unearth the visible features and the underlying intricacies that shape your home's narrative. Every crack, every flaw, and every functional aspect is meticulously examined, culminating in a comprehensive report that outlines your property's strengths and vulnerabilities. Armed with this invaluable knowledge, you step into home selling with a clear understanding of your property's condition, enabling you to make informed decisions.

However, the true power of preemptive inspections goes beyond knowledge; it lies in preparation. By unveiling potential issues upfront, you gain the upper hand in a process often rife with negotiations. By addressing those minor repairs in advance, you position your property as one that is not only visually appealing but also structurally sound, eliminating potential concerns. This level of preparation isn't just about enhancing your property's marketability; it's about fostering confidence among potential buyers and preemptively thwarting negotiations centered around repairs during the critical escrow period.

The benefits of a preemptive inspection ripple through the entire home-selling journey, but its impact doesn't stop there. It's a testament to your dedication to transparency, commitment to a smooth transaction, and foresight in anticipating potential obstacles. As you welcome potential buyers into your home, you're offering them not just a property but a meticulously vetted haven—a space that's been thoroughly examined and thoughtfully prepared.

Preemptive Inspections: Roadmap for a Seamless Sale

Imagine a clear road map, illuminating every twist and turn ahead. That is precisely what a preemptive home inspection provides—a roadmap of your property's condition, enabling you to address any potential issues before they become negotiating points during the sale process. You comprehensively understand your home's strengths and vulnerabilities by conducting a thorough home inspection.

These preemptive inspections may include a general home inspection which covers multiple facets of the home, pest and termite inspection, roof inspection, and, if applicable, a septic tank inspection or an inspection of your pool and jacuzzi if you have them. Armed with this knowledge, you not only make informed decisions but also have the opportunity to proactively attend to any necessary repairs. By addressing these issues upfront, you enhance your home's appeal to potential buyers and eliminate the risk of negotiations revolving around repair requests during the escrow period. Preparing in this manner establishes you as a confident and transparent seller, fostering trust and often expediting the closing process.

Decoding Your Home's Value: Appraisals vs. Comparative Market Analysis

In the intricate realm of discerning the true value of your home, two pivotal tools come to the forefront: appraisals and comparative market analyses (CMAs). These tools act as windows, allowing you to peer into the multifaceted pricing landscape and providing invaluable insights that can mold your strategic selling approach. As we delve into the heart of these tools, we'll uncover the distinctions that can significantly influence your decision-making process. To explore how these insights shape the art of pricing, read Chapter 8: The Price is Right: Strategic Pricing for Maximum Profit.

Appraisal: Precise Evaluation by a Certified Appraiser

Imagine your home under the expert gaze of a trained professional—a certified appraiser whose mission is to unearth every facet contributing to its value. This meticulous evaluation delves beyond the surface, considering your property's physical condition, features, and recent comparable sales. The result? An unbiased market value, meticulously calculated to reflect the true worth of your home.

Certified appraisers are skilled at parsing through data, identifying trends, and understanding the unique characteristics that set your property apart. This professional assessment carries significant weight and is often demanded by lenders, ensuring that the sale price aligns with the authentic value of the property. It's a safeguard that adds credibility to your pricing strategy and assures buyers and lenders that your home's value is grounded in expertise.

Comparative Market Analysis: A Gauge of Market Trends

While an appraisal takes a deep dive into the intricacies of your property, the comparative market analysis (CMA) operates on a different plane—a more holistic view of the market's pulse. Conducted by a licensed real estate agent, a CMA analyzes recently sold properties in your area to provide an estimated market value.

This tool taps into the power of trends and collective behavior, offering a snapshot of how properties similar to yours are faring in the market. While a CMA doesn't delve solely into the granular details of your property's physical condition, it does offer an invaluable gauge of your property's worth based on the broader landscape.

It's crucial to recognize that while both tools provide insights, they serve different purposes. An appraisal delivers a precise and comprehensive evaluation, while a CMA offers a more fluid understanding of your property's position within the market's ebb and flow. While both tools are valuable, lenders place weight on the appraised value to ensure buyers do not overpay what the property is worth.

Understanding these distinctions empowers you to make informed decisions to set the perfect price for your property. By leveraging the insights gained from a certified appraisal and a real estate agent's CMA, you equip yourself with a well-rounded perspective that can guide your pricing strategy and ultimately lead to a successful sale.

Mastering Expert Repairs: Elevating Your Property's Allure

Investing in expert repairs is one of the most compelling ways to elevate your property's appeal. Whether addressing a leaky roof, upgrading electrical systems, or enhancing the curb appeal, expert repairs showcase your dedication to presenting a well-maintained and desirable property.

By addressing repairs before listing, you clearly message potential buyers that your home has been cared for and is move-in ready. Moreover, expert repairs can justify a higher asking price, as buyers recognize the value in not having to undertake immediate maintenance tasks upon purchase.

The Triumphant Trio: Inspections, Appraisals, and Repairs

In home selling, navigating inspections, appraisals, and expert repairs forms a triumphant trio that sets the stage for a seamless and successful transaction. By conducting preemptive inspections, understanding the nuances of appraisals, and investing in expert repairs, you're taking proactive control of your selling journey.

Embrace these professional services as tools that empower you to present your property in the best possible light, address potential hurdles, and maximize your selling potential. With the insights gained from inspections, the accuracy of certified appraisals, and the allure of expert repairs, you're not just selling a property—you're offering a meticulously crafted home that resonates with confidence and value.

CHAPTER 6

Investing Wisely:
Upgrades That Skyrocket a Home's Value

Now it's time to focus your attention on the influence of strategic upgrades—an arena where every investment promises to elevate your home's value and visual appeal. Imagine yourself at the pivotal juncture of decision-making, presented with an array of upgrade options. Throughout this transformative exploration, we'll dive extensively into the craft of astute investment, guaranteeing that your endeavors yield significant rewards.

The Art of Value-Adding Upgrades

When you're a homeowner preparing to sell, it's easy to be captivated by the allure of renovations. The dream of a remodeled kitchen, a luxurious bathroom, or a beautifully landscaped backyard can spark your imagination. However, it's essential to remember that not all upgrades are equal in terms of adding value to your home. Wise investment is the key.

Consider this scenario: You decide to embark on an $100,000 kitchen remodel. It includes state-of-the-art appliances, custom cabinetry, and luxurious countertops. The transformation is undoubtedly breathtaking, and it elevates the aesthetics of your home. However, it's important to understand that the entire $100,000 investment may not translate dollar-for-dollar into your home's appraised value.

While these upgrades are impactful, they often contribute only a fraction of their total cost when your home is appraised.

To maximize your home's value, focus on improvements that strike a balance between aesthetics and practicality. For the kitchen, consider modernizing your countertops with materials like granite, quartz, or marble. These not only look appealing but also offer durability and are likely to recoup a significant portion of the investment.

A mosaic tile backsplash is another kitchen upgrade that can make a big difference. It adds a touch of elegance and can transform the overall look. Fresh paint on the walls and cabinets can provide a cost-effective facelift, making the space feel bright and inviting.

In the bathroom, updating the countertops with quality materials like granite or quartz can enhance both visual appeal and functionality. New fixtures, including faucets and showerheads are cost effective and can provide a contemporary feel. Additionally, a fresh coat of paint can work wonders in creating a clean and well-maintained appearance.

Don't underestimate the value of deep cleaning your appliances and fixtures; by doing so, you can save on buying and installing new fixtures. A sparkling clean kitchen and bathroom convey a sense of pride in homeownership and can leave a lasting impression on potential buyers.

It's crucial to strike a balance between investing in upgrades and the expected return on investment. While lavish remodels can be enticing, remember that not all improvements yield a dollar-for-dollar return. Prioritize upgrades that enhance the overall appeal, functionality, and cleanliness of these key areas, as they are more likely to attract potential buyers and maximize your home's value..

The Importance of Curb Appeal: Welcoming First Impressions

Amidst the array of upgrades, a cornerstone of value enhancement rests in the realm of curb appeal—a vital first chapter in the story of your home. The power of curb appeal lies in those initial moments when potential buyers first set eyes on your property. It's the symphony of visual cues that evoke emotions, set expectations, and shape perceptions.

Consider this: a modest investment, perhaps as little as $5 to $10 per cobblestone, can transform your front yard into a canvas of beauty. A simple cobblestone path meandering through lush grass leading to the garage can evoke a sense of charm and sophistication. It's a subtle yet impactful detail that showcases thoughtfulness and care.

But it's not just about pathways. Flower beds, often overlooked, can become radiant focal points with a little attention. Cleaning and refreshing flower beds, combined with the strategic addition of year-round succulents, create an evergreen burst of color. Buyers envision themselves nurturing a vibrant garden, and this vibrant image can nudge them toward a positive emotional connection.

Drought-Resistant Landscaping: A Sustainable Marvel

In the era of sustainability, the concept of drought-resistant landscaping stands as a compelling upgrade. Transforming your yard into a haven of water-efficient greenery aligns with eco-conscious trends and offers practical benefits. Drought-resistant plants, meticulously chosen for their endurance and beauty, adorn your landscape with bursts of life while minimizing water consumption.

Imagine the allure of a yard that remains lush and vibrant even in the face of water restrictions. This transformation sends a powerful message - a message of responsible living and long-term value. Potential buyers recognize the appeal of a yard that demands minimal maintenance and water resources, fostering a connection between sustainability and property value.

Understanding the Return on Investment (ROI)

The concept of return on investment (ROI) is your compass in the realm of upgrades. ROI measures the ratio between the cost of an upgrade and the increase in your property's value. In essence, it gauges the effectiveness of an investment in terms of its impact on your bottom line.

As mentioned previously, a kitchen remodel may not recoup the entire investment; however, it can still enhance your property's appeal and attract potential buyers. The key is to focus on upgrades that offer a balance between cost and value increase. Updates that improve functionality, aesthetics, and energy efficiency tend to yield higher returns.

Striking the Balance

As you embark on your upgrade journey, strike a balance between your vision and market demands. While personalization is important, remember that buyers seek a canvas upon which to paint their own dreams. Aim for upgrades that are neutral, timeless, and widely appealing.

When it comes to selling your home, every dollar invested should have the potential to yield returns that align with your goals. Investing wisely is about understanding the nuances of your market, recognizing the impact of each upgrade, and striking the delicate balance between personalization and market appeal. By navigating this path with insight and discernment, you're setting the stage for a home-selling journey where every upgrade shines.

CHAPTER 7

The Agent Advantage:
Leverage Professionals for Top Dollar Sale

This chapter will unveil the transformative partnership between homeowners and real estate professionals. This partnership holds the key to unlocking your property's full potential and maximizing your profit margins. The following pages discuss the art of leveraging expert guidance to propel your home sale toward unmatched success. However, before we delve into the advantages of such a partnership, let's take a closer look at the challenges and complexities that come with selling a home on your own, often referred to as FSBO (For Sale By Owner).

Selling a home on your own can be challenging, requiring significant time, effort, and expertise, also referred to as FSBO (For Sale By Owner). When opting for FSBO, homeowners take on the responsibilities typically handled by real estate professionals. This includes pricing the property accurately, marketing it effectively, navigating legal and contractual intricacies, managing legal disclosures, and negotiating with potential buyers.

To successfully sell a home as an FSBO, you'll need to start by conducting thorough market research to determine a competitive and attractive listing price. You'll also need to create compelling marketing materials to showcase your home's features, including photographs and property descriptions. You will also be responsible for handling inquiries, scheduling showings, and managing the intricacies of real estate contracts and negotiations.

Furthermore, FSBO sellers should be prepared to invest time in promoting their property through various online and offline channels to reach a broad audience of potential buyers. While selling your home on your own is possible, it often requires a deep understanding of the real estate market, a significant time commitment, and the willingness to personally manage all aspects of the sale.

In contrast, partnering with a seasoned real estate professional can offer valuable expertise, market insights, and a network of potential buyers that can streamline the selling process and potentially lead to a more profitable sale. The proceeding sections of this chapter will delve into the advantages of working with a real estate agent and how this partnership can maximize your return on investment.

A Strategic Symphony: Real Estate Agents and You

Imagine the fusion of your property's unique essence with the expertise of a seasoned real estate agent—a professional equipped with a symphony of negotiation skills, marketing prowess, and a profound understanding of market dynamics. Together, you're a dynamic duo poised to navigate the intricate pathways of home selling, maximizing every opportunity along the way.

Mastering the Art of Negotiation and Marketing

Beyond the realm of services, real estate agents are masters of negotiation—a skill set that can directly impact your profit potential. Their adeptness in securing seller discounts for services like staging, repairs, and other enhancements ensures that your investments generate higher returns. This strategic approach positions your property as a potential canvas for buyers, compelling them to see its worth.

In the world of marketing, real estate agents wield unparalleled power. The Multiple Listing Service (MLS), an expansive digital platform, becomes a stage where your property is showcased to a global audience. With carefully curated listings enriched by captivating imagery and compelling narratives, your property shines as a star amidst the constellation of offerings, attracting buyers from near and far.

The Spark of Seller-Deferred Renovation Programs

In recent years, one of the most intriguing strategies offered by real estate agents is the seller deferred renovation program—a catalyst for success that transforms your property into a masterpiece. This ingenious program grants you the ability to pursue upgrades that range from small fixes to major transformations, such as kitchen and bathroom renovations, full home painting, meticulous landscaping, and expert staging.

Seller Deferred Renovations are a revolutionary approach that blends vision with financial prudence. This program empowers you to embark on essential upgrades, ranging from rejuvenating a tired kitchen to crafting an oasis-like bathroom. It's the transformational magic of a fresh coat of paint enveloping your entire home or the allure of meticulously landscaped gardens that whisper a promise of serenity.

The brilliance of the deferred renovation program lies in its ability to illuminate your property's full potential without immediate financial strain. The majority of the programs offered through an agent's partnership do not require upfront costs, credit checks or deposits before listing your home for sale; and it gives you leverage to upgrade and pay at closing.

Further, these programs are most suitable for property owners who have positive equity in their homes. You can expect to have a personally assigned project manager, a licensed and bonded general contractor and a team of experienced craftsman to assist you each step of the way during renovations. As you invest in upgrades that amplify your property's appeal, the costs are deferred until the sale is concluded. By taking this approach, buyers are offered a glimpse of your property's potential without the concern of wondering how long it will be before they can occupy their new residence.

A Network of Expertise and Insight

Real estate agents bring a treasure trove of expertise that transcends conventional boundaries. Their intricate understanding of buyer behavior empowers them to position your property in a way that resonates deeply with your target audience. Guided by their insights, you make informed decisions that elevate your selling strategy and amplify its impact.

Moreover, their extensive network is a tapestry of connections, ranging from trusted contractors for repairs to staging professionals who transform spaces into showcases. With their guidance, your property evolves into an oasis of allure, its every facet reflecting a harmonious blend of strategic vision and expert execution.

Agent Commission: Navigating Costs and Negotiations

While we are delving into leveraging the expertise of professional estate agents, let's get the topic of commissions out of the way.

Regarding the compensation of real estate agents, it is essential to understand that agent commissions are not fixed in concrete terms.. The National Association of Realtors affirms that agent commissions are negotiable and essentially set by the local real estate markets based on consumer preference, services provided, and what the market can bear, among other factors (1). This means that while industry standards exist, the actual commission rate can vary.

Agent commissions encompass more than just the percentage negotiated. Real estate professionals often assume significant upfront costs to effectively market your property and expedite the selling process. The extent of these expenses can vary based on the level of services your agent provides. For a standard non-luxury home, you can anticipate upfront costs ranging from $3,500 and beyond. In contrast, luxury homes and residential income properties may incur even higher marketing expenses, reaching anywhere from $5,000 to $20,000 or more. These expenses represent the initial investment made by the agent to guarantee your property receives the attention it truly deserves..

Now, let's break down how commissions work. In a typical listing agreement, the seller agrees to pay a total commission, often around 6% of the final sales price. The commission is divided between the listing and buying brokerage offices. However, it doesn't stop there; the commission is further divided between each brokerage to pay the agents involved.

Understanding that the agent doesn't receive the entire commission is important. Instead, it's split multiple ways. From the commission earned, the agent covers a multitude of expenses, including the upfront marketing, incurred costs associated with hosting open houses, transaction coordination fees, liability insurance, coordinating the escrow and closing, coordinating inspections and viewings, responding to all inquiries, time spent in negotiations, managing legal documents, and paying taxes among other things. These costs are part of the comprehensive service experienced real estate professionals provide to ensure a successful sale that fetches top dollar.

In some instances, you might be able to negotiate a lower commission in a scenario known as "dual agency." If it is allowed in your state, dual agency is when the listing agent is also representing a buyer who may have contacted them directly from the listing advertisement. On this occasion, you may be able to add a clause in your listing agreement stating a lower fee will be paid to the listing brokerage if the agent represents both you and the buyer (2).

Agents are highly motivated to help you sell your home. If your home does not sell, the agents do not receive a commission, potentially resulting in the loss of thousands of dollars from their efforts. Finally, agents are independent contractors and the majority of brokerages they work for do not cover these prelisting expenses as some may think. Therefore, when you enlist the expertise of a professional real estate agent, they are committed to your highest interests and motivated to help you sell your home as quickly and efficiently as possible.

The Agent Advantage: A Symphony of Success

As you take the home selling journey, the agent advantage emerges as a symphony of success—a harmonious blend of your aspirations and the proficiency of real estate professionals. This partnership magnifies every decision, strategy, and investment, amplifying their impact and steering your sales toward top-dollar success.

Remember, the agent advantage is more than a practical choice—it's an investment in expertise, insight, and guidance. By aligning your path with the prowess of real estate professionals, you're securing a home-selling journey marked by strategic intent, informed decisions, and a symphony of success.

Sources:
(1) https://cdn.nar.realtor/sites/default/files/documents/how-real-estate-commissions-work-2022-08-01.pdf
(2) https://www.realtor.com/advice/sell/how-to-negotiate-a-realtor-commission/

CHAPTER 8

The Price is Right:
Strategic Pricing for Maximum Profit

As we explore the realm of pricing, we uncover a pivotal art—
one that wields the power to influence the outcome of your
home sale. In this section, we demystify the delicate balance
between perception and reality, unveiling the intricacies of
strategic pricing that can generate significant buyer interest and
potentially spark a bidding frenzy for your property.

Pricing: Beyond Numbers, Into Psychology

The journey of pricing your home isn't merely an exercise in
mathematics—it's a symphony of psychology and strategy.
The price tag attached to your property serves as an invitation
to prospective buyers, offering a glimpse into the value they
stand to gain. As such, striking the right chord becomes
essential to evoke curiosity, excitement, and a sense of
urgency.

Imagine this: Your property is priced just below its perceived
value, capturing the attention of a wide pool of buyers. This
strategic move sparks a competitive atmosphere, with multiple
interested parties vying for the opportunity to secure your
home. This phenomenon, known as a bidding war, transforms
your selling journey into an exhilarating experience, potentially
leading to an offer that surpasses your initial expectations.

Initiating the Bidding Frenzy:

In the realm of strategic pricing, an astute move is to position your home as an enticing prospect, priced to attract a multitude of potential buyers. The objective is to kindle interest and stimulate action, prompting buyers to envision themselves in your property. This approach generates a buzz of anticipation, with buyers recognizing the unique opportunity to secure a highly coveted property.

The bidding war, a result of strategic pricing, unveils a landscape where prospective buyers are driven to outbid each other. This spirited competition not only elevates your property's perceived value but also often leads to offers that exceed your initial asking price. The orchestration of this bidding frenzy rests on the careful calibration of your property's price—a balance between enticing offers and stoking competition.

Intelligent Pricing: The Sweet Spot

Intelligent pricing forms the bedrock of your strategic selling approach—it's the delicate balancing act that harmonizes your property's value with the ebb and flow of the market. As you delve into the art of pricing, consider positioning your property just below market value. This calculated strategy not only captures attention but also beckons potential buyers, creating a favorable backdrop for competitive offers. Visualize this phenomenon through the lens of diagram #1—a visual representation of the "sweet spot" that places your home in a realm that both entices and encapsulates its genuine worth.

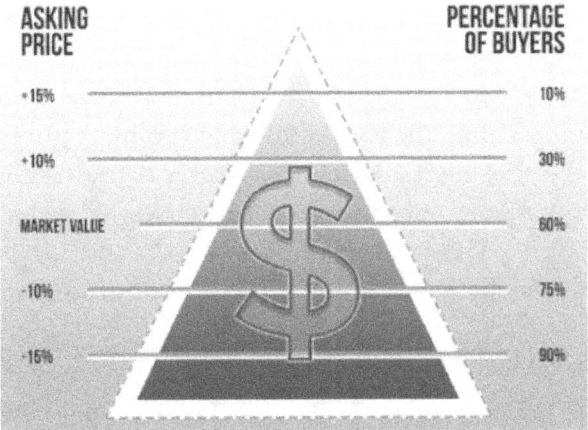

ASKING PRICE / PERCENTAGE OF BUYERS

ASKING PRICE	PERCENTAGE OF BUYERS
+ 15%	10%
+ 10%	30%
MARKET VALUE	60%
- 10%	75%
- 15%	90%

Diagram #1: Intelligent Pricing Strategy Framework

The numbers on diagram #1—suggesting a reduction of 15% to 10% below market value—might appear substantial at first glance, depending on the variables within your specific market. You want to engage in a comprehensive discussion of this strategy with your trusted real estate agent to ensure you don't inadvertently leave money on the table. Expert guidance is critical to navigating the nuances of your market's potential and avoiding missed opportunities.

Central to this discussion is the notion of fair market value—a value that arises from the consensus between a willing buyer and seller, underlined by a contractual agreement. While many factors can influence values, location and condition emerge as the predominant determinants. Comparative analysis of other similar properties that have recently sold or are currently listed within your vicinity generally shapes fair market value.

Approaching pricing strategically mandates a profound comprehension of your local market dynamics, recent transaction data, and the prevailing sentiments of potential buyers. This intricate tapestry of information requires collaboration with your real estate agent, the expert who can assist in pinpointing the ideal initial price point. A price that not only garners interest but incites a magnetic attraction—drawing buyers to your property with an irresistible allure. This allure, in turn, paves the way for negotiations and, ideally, a competitive bidding war that maximizes your profit potential.

Remember, the objective transcends mere offers—kindling a fire of fervent interest, igniting the competitive spirit among buyers, and ultimately reaping the rewards of a strategically priced property.

The Timing Truisms: The First Two Weeks

As you set foot on the path of pricing your home, there are enduring realities that should never be underestimated. Central to this endeavor is the concept of fair market value—an essential guiding principle that magnetizes potential buyers, while an excessive price tag can deter them. This can be visualized through the lens of Diagram #2, where the first two weeks emerge as a pivotal juncture in your home-selling journey.

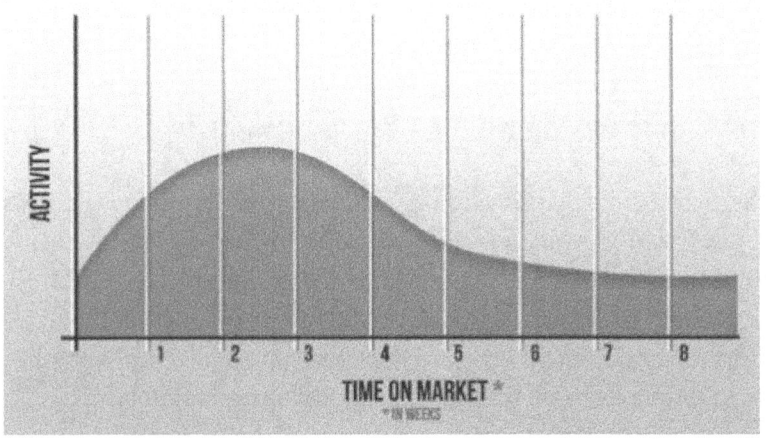

Diagram #2: Intelligent Pricing Strategy Framework

Consider this timeframe as the initial phase of your home sale—an opportune moment that captures the attention of both buyers and their agents. Diagram #2 aptly illustrates the pattern of these early weeks, comparable to a surge in activity. With your property featured on various platforms, including local listings and online portals like the Multiple Listing Service, it generates a flurry of curiosity and interest. The momentum gained during this phase holds the potential to stimulate bidding wars, ultimately increasing your chances of achieving a more substantial return on your investment.

Adapt and Enhance: Valuable Feedback

If showings and offers are scarce during this initial phase, it's time to heed the valuable feedback that the market provides. This is where your real estate agent's expertise shines—consult with them to explore possibilities for enhancing your home's curb appeal or staging its interior to greater advantage.

Remember, the market offers insights to refine your approach and help your property shine.

The Future of Opportunity: Price Adjustments

The market is a dynamic entity that can shift its course, but the key is not to let precious time slip away. While the market can offer a second chance, it's crucial to avoid delays that could cloud your property's value. Intelligent pricing isn't solely about maximizing profit—it's about positioning your home to be sold quickly and efficiently while still commanding its fair market value.

In the journey of selling your home, pricing emerges as a strategic art form that can determine the trajectory of your sale. Collaborate with your real estate agent to decode the market's language, offering your property at a price that entices buyers and fuels a competitive atmosphere. By mastering this art, you're unlocking the potential for maximum profit and a triumphant selling experience.

The Catalyst for a Successful Sale

Strategic pricing isn't merely about numbers—it's about triggering a chain reaction of interest, inquiries, and offers, culminating in a successful sale. You're laying the groundwork for a swift and lucrative transaction by positioning your property as an irresistible proposition. The outcome? A property that commands the attention of serious buyers, resulting in an atmosphere where offers unfold like a symphony.

As you focus on pricing your home, remember it's not a solitary decision. Work with an experienced real estate agent who has an understanding of the market and ready to help you achieve top dollars for your home. Together, you can work towards a pricing strategy that effectively aligns with your specific goals and objectives. By setting the stage for a bidding war through strategic pricing, you're forging a path that leads to maximum profit and a triumphant home-selling journey.

CHAPTER 9

Pricing Precision:
The Dangers of Overpricing Your Home

In the intricate puzzle of real estate, each home stands as a unique piece, revealing its distinct value in the grand tapestry of a neighborhood. What makes one home worth more than another, even within a sea of similar houses? The answer lies in a delicate interplay of variables that have fascinated buyers and sellers for generations. Let's delve into pricing precision, where the significance of your home's value is revealed.

When a home transitions from seller to buyer, it signifies a significant change. The home's value is established through the agreement between willing parties; the seller and buyer. This transaction serves as a benchmark for other comparable homes, but it's only the beginning. Various fundamental factors continue to shape the value proposition of each dwelling:

Location: The proximity of a home to essential amenities such as workplaces, parks, transportation hubs, schools, and community services significantly influences its desirability. A prime location enhances the value, making it a prized asset for potential buyers.

Size: Square footage holds rank in determining home values, as larger homes require more building materials and offer increased living space. A larger lot provides added privacy, another desirable trait affecting perceived value.

Number of Bedrooms and Baths: As time progresses, societal preferences evolve. Today, families seek greater privacy, resulting in a taste for homes with multiple bedrooms and bathrooms. The average home purchased now often boasts three bedrooms and two baths, reflecting contemporary family dynamics.

Features and Finishes: Luxurious features such as outdoor kitchens and spa-like bathrooms can elevate a home's value. Details like hardwood floors and granite countertops signify higher quality and command a premium over homes with more basic finishes.

Condition: The age and condition of a home contribute significantly to its value. Modern homes resembling new constructions tend to retain their value better, as they exude a sense of being up-to-date, safe, and appealing. Homes that require updates or exhibit poor maintenance tend to sell for less.

Curb Appeal: The first impression matters, and curb appeal plays a vital role in shaping that initial perception. A well-maintained exterior, enhanced by fresh landscaping and vibrant flowers, adds charm and allure to the property.

Even among two seemingly identical homes within the same neighborhood, subtle distinctions can result in differences in pricing. A breathtaking view, a carefully chosen color palette, or the distinct personal touches of the homeowner can all influence the perceived value.

Yet, valuing a home is not a precise science but an art influenced by myriad factors. While the puzzle may never be perfectly assembled, making informed decisions can safeguard your investment. Wise purchases, coupled with consistent updates and meticulous maintenance, enable homeowners to recoup a substantial portion, if not the entirety, of their investment.

However, pricing a home comes with its pitfalls, and one of the most common traps is overpricing. This perilous misstep is often fueled by sellers who view their homes through a sentimental lens, believing that a higher initial price can be lowered later if necessary. Yet, this inclination can prove to be a grave miscalculation.

Overpricing operates as a barrier, shielding your home from the very eyes of eligible buyers, and ranks #3 of the top three reasons homes do not sell. Potential buyers typically browse within specific price ranges, seeking the best value within those confines. An inflated price tag alienates your home from these discerning buyers, deterring them from even considering it as an option.

The repercussions of overpricing extend far beyond mere initial impressions. Real estate agents are often cautious about listing homes at inflated prices because they know it can deter potential buyers. When a home is priced above what the market deems reasonable, it can languish on the market for extended periods without showings or offers, creating the perception that something might be wrong with the property. In some cases, the listing might even expire, inadvertently sending the message that the property is unsellable or problematic.

It's crucial to recognize a delicate balance in pricing a home. The three primary points to consider are as follows:

1. Below Market Value: This strategy often sparks competitive bidding wars among potential buyers, increasing your chances of securing multiple offers.

2. At Market Value: Pricing your home in line with market standards positions it competitively, attracting interested buyers who perceive its value.

3. Above Market Value: Opting for a price above market value can discourage potential buyers, limiting their interest and offers.

Understanding these pricing dynamics can help you avoid overpricing pitfalls and make a strategic decision that aligns with your selling goals.

Ultimately, the reasons homes don't sell are overpricing, inadequate exposure, and limited accessibility which stand as a stark reminder of the perils that accompany misaligned pricing strategies. You eliminate one of these barriers by pricing your home intelligently, ensuring your property resonates with the right audience and stands poised for a successful sale.

CHAPTER 10

Transforming Your Space: Decluttering and Depersonalizing

First impressions yield a unique power—they possess the ability to instantly captivate potential buyers, creating a lasting imprint of a property's potential. Imagine walking into a home that beckons with open arms, where every room resonates with an air of possibility. It's a canvas upon which buyers can paint their dreams, and the strategic art of decluttering and depersonalizing intricately weaves this transformational magic.

Decluttering: Clearing the Path to Imagination

Decluttering isn't merely about organizing your belongings; it's an art form that paves the way to a harmonious and inviting space. It's a conscious choice to create an atmosphere of tranquility by carefully selecting what stays and what goes. The journey starts with embracing the essence of "less is more," a philosophy that can be emotionally challenging for those who hold sentimental value in their possessions.

This is where professional home organizers emerge as invaluable allies. Their expertise extends beyond mere tidying; they collaborate with you to make informed decisions on what stays and what can be donated, sold, or discarded. The process is methodical, categorizing items into four distinct groups: those to be kept, donated, sold, or disposed of. Items that no longer serve you find a new purpose in being donated to charity, infusing goodwill into your journey. If you're inclined, hosting a yard sale or estate sale offers another avenue to part ways with items that have overstayed their welcome.

In the spirit of decluttering, addressing items that no longer serve a functional purpose is crucial. Items that are damaged, broken, or unusable should gracefully find their way to the realm of disposables. Not only does this enhance the visual allure of your home, but it also enables potential buyers to visualize their own lives flourishing within the space. In fact, a clutter-free environment creates an illusion of spaciousness, transforming rooms into welcoming havens.

As you navigate the terrain of decluttering, one practical strategy takes center stage and that's the use effective use of space transformation. This phase isn't just about getting rid of excess items; it's about crafting an environment that allows potential buyers to envision their future in your home.

Depersonalizing: Crafting a Blank Canvas for Dreams

Depersonalizing is a dance of subtlety—a process that involves carefully tucking away personal memorabilia to usher in a neutral, open canvas. The goal is to create an environment where potential buyers can seamlessly project their aspirations onto the space. By removing personalized touches, you allow room for others to dream.

One of the key elements of depersonalizing involves storing away family photos, heirlooms, and personalized decor. This pivotal step sets the stage for potential buyers to envisage their own stories unfolding within these walls. While it's essential to maintain a sense of warmth through selective decorative pieces, the focus remains on establishing a clean, neutral atmosphere that welcomes everyone.

A critical facet of depersonalization is recognizing the value of safeguarding your possessions, especially those of immense personal and financial value. Ensuring the security of your valuables during the home-selling process is a crucial responsibility that falls squarely on your shoulders. Remember, real estate agents are not accountable for any lost or stolen items left unattended during open houses or showings. You must take the necessary precautions to protect your valuable belongings.

Consider the advantage of using external storage options as a safe place to temporarily store your treasures. Whether you choose PODS, CubeSmart, Public Storage, or opt for the secure confines of a safety deposit box for your valuable jewelry, these solutions provide a layer of protection during this transitional period.

Another practical approach is utilizing your garage or a secluded room to store items you're not using. However, it's important to weigh this choice against the potential impact on viewing accessibility. While it might seem convenient, remember that cluttering up these spaces could hinder buyers from fully appreciating your home's features.

Beyond just tidying up, the process of decluttering and depersonalizing serves a pragmatic purpose. It's about minimizing distractions and maximizing your property's potential. Thoughtfully curating your space allows your home's best features to shine. This means creating a neutral backdrop that enables potential buyers to imagine their own lives fitting seamlessly into the space.

In addition to organizing and tidying, consider the security of items like expensive jewelry and heirlooms. These valuable possessions should be stored safely, out of sight, and reach during open houses or showings. Realize that this responsibility rests squarely on the seller to protect your valuables.

Ultimately, decluttering and depersonalizing are more than just practical steps; they're essential elements of a successful home sale. Presenting a clean, organized, and welcoming space allows potential buyers to picture themselves living in your home. Remember, the goal is to showcase your home's potential and let its features shine while creating a safe environment and inviting for all parties involved.

The subsequent chapter will discuss the transformative journey of preparing your home to shine. This chapter details the steps to captivate buyers' attention, unleash their imagination, and ultimately craft the stage for a triumphant showcase.

CHAPTER 11

Setting the Stage for Success: Preparing Your Home to Shine

Crafting a captivating first impression is paramount. The moment potential buyers' step through your doorway, their experience can set the tone for their entire walk-through. Enter the art of staging—a transformative process that goes beyond simple aesthetics. Staging involves carefully orchestrating your home's layout, decor, and ambiance to ignite the imagination of potential buyers. This chapter is your guide to the enchanting world of staging, revealing the steps to prepare your home to radiate its most compelling charm and allure.

Creating an Irresistible Ambiance: The Essence of Staging

Staging is more than just embellishing your living space; it's about creating an irresistible ambiance that sparks emotions. By decluttering and depersonalizing, you enable potential buyers to envision themselves inhabiting your home. This emotional connection is a driving force in their decision-making process.

The Choreography of Arrangement: Furniture Placement as Art

Staging transcends mere furniture arrangement; it's similar to choreographing a captivating dance that guides buyers seamlessly through your home. Each room should flow organically, allowing buyers to imagine how they would inhabit the space. The positioning of furniture, the arrangement of decor, and the interplay of light all contribute to a harmonious experience.

The Power of Neutral Tones: A Canvas for Imagination

Neutral tones are like a blank canvas for potential buyers to paint their dreams upon. When selecting colors, opt for soft and muted tones that provide a versatile backdrop for personalization while also appealing to a broad range of preferences.

The beauty of neutrals lies in their adaptability. Soft whites, warm grays, gentle beige, and subtle pastels create an atmosphere of tranquility and sophistication. These colors don't impose a particular style or taste on the viewer, allowing them to envision their own furniture, decor, and personal touches in the space.

Neutral tones have a timeless quality that transcends trends. They create a sense of continuity and flow throughout your home, making it feel cohesive and well put together. Potential buyers can more easily visualize themselves living in a space when it provides a neutral foundation for their own ideas and styles.

Moreover, neutral colors are less likely to clash with a buyer's existing furniture and belongings. They offer a sense of calm and space, making rooms appear larger and more inviting. This appeal to a wide range of tastes and the sense of expansiveness can increase your home's desirability and marketability.

When staging your home with neutral tones, consider light-colored walls, neutral flooring, and soft furnishings. These elements combine to create a serene and harmonious environment that encourages potential buyers to imagine their life within your home.

Engaging All the Senses: Subtle Impact of the Atmosphere

Staging isn't solely visual—it's an experience that engages all the senses. Consider playing calming music in the background to cultivate a relaxing atmosphere. Subtle scents, like the aroma of fresh flowers or baked goods, can create a welcoming environment that lingers in the minds of buyers.

Embracing Outdoor Elegance: Extending the Appeal

Your outdoor spaces are an extension of your home's charm. Don't underestimate their potential. Well-maintained gardens, inviting seating arrangements, and thoughtful accents enhance your property's overall appeal. These spaces allow potential buyers to visualize themselves enjoying outdoor living, making your property even more enticing.

Expert Staging Consultation: Elevating Your Presentation

For a polished touch, consider enlisting a professional stager's expertise. They bring fresh perspectives and a refined eye for detail to your staging process. Some real estate agents may even provide staging as a premium service, with the option for complimentary or deferred payment based on the extent of required staging. A professional stager maximizes your home's strengths and minimizes its weaknesses, crafting a harmonious presentation that resonates with potential buyers.

Creating Brilliance on a Budget: Staging on Your Terms

Even if staging services are beyond your budget, there are myriad ways to enhance your home's appeal. Start by giving your bathroom and kitchen a deep clean. Ordinary household items like baking soda can transform faucets and stovetops to glisten. Cleaning carpets, washing windows, and washing curtains can bring renewed freshness. Address pet odors, refresh sofa cushions, trim the lawn and power wash outdoor areas to create an inviting atmosphere.

Ambiance of Smell: A Subtle Scent of Invitation

In the realm of home staging, where every sensory detail plays a pivotal role, the significance of scent should not be underestimated. Beyond the visual and auditory aspects, the sense of smell plays a crucial role in crafting a welcoming and inviting atmosphere within your home. As you prepare your property to shine, addressing household odors becomes a vital consideration. One effective approach is to use neutral-scented plug-ins that gently infuse your home with a welcoming aroma.

However, it's equally essential to address any unpleasant odors that may linger in your home, as these can significantly influence the perception of potential buyers when they step inside. These unwanted scents can emanate from various sources, such as pets, garbage, dirty laundry, mildew in bathrooms, or even the garage, and can detract from the overall appeal of your property. Therefore, it's crucial to be vigilant in managing and banishing these odors, ensuring that your living spaces remain odor-free and inviting.

Implementing effective strategies to maintain a fresh environment is essential. For instance, if you have pets, thorough cleaning of their living areas and the use of air purifiers can help minimize pet odors. Regularly emptying garbage bins and ensuring proper ventilation in various areas of your home will prevent lingering odors. Additionally, paying particular attention to moisture-prone areas and mildew prevention will significantly enhance the overall ambiance of your home.

Beyond eliminating unpleasant odors, consider introducing subtle scents that evoke comfort and warmth, further elevating the overall sensory experience for potential buyers. A bowl of potpourri, scented candles, or reed diffusers can infuse your space with a gentle fragrance. Opting for universally pleasant scents like lavender, vanilla, or citrus can create an inviting atmosphere that resonates with a wide range of preferences.

Aromas possess a unique ability to elicit emotions and awaken memories, fostering a lasting and positive connection between prospective buyers and your home. Deliberately choosing delightful scents contributes to this emotional bond and leaves a lasting impression. However, while incorporating scents, it's essential to strike a harmonious balance, ensuring that the aroma complements rather than overwhelms the overall ambiance created through staging. Light, pleasant, and universally appealing scents are key to achieving this balance and appealing to a diverse range of potential buyers.

Embracing Scent as a Dimension of Staging: The Final Touch

As you journey home staging, consider scent as an integral dimension of the process. Just as carefully curated decor and strategic furniture placement create an inviting environment, a subtle and pleasant aroma can enhance the overall sensory experience. By thoughtfully managing household smells and introducing gentle scents, you create a multi-dimensional atmosphere that envelops potential buyers in comfort and allure.

Incorporating this aspect into your home-selling journey is another way to ensure your property resonates positively with potential buyers. It's a testament to your dedication to presenting your home in the best light, addressing what meets the eye and engages the senses. As you craft an environment that appeals to every facet of your audience, you're taking a step closer to a successful sale.

Staging is like the conductor of an orchestral masterpiece—it harmonizes a seamless experience for potential buyers. A well-staged home doesn't merely present—it showcases the lifestyle it offers, enabling buyers to visualize themselves within its walls. Staging isn't about masking your home—it's about enhancing its beauty, magnifying its potential, and cultivating an atmosphere that resonates with diverse tastes. By embracing staging, you're setting the stage for success, presenting your property as an irresistible vision that beckons a swift and rewarding sale. Whether through professional expertise or personal touches, staging empowers you to create a stage where your home truly shines.

CHAPTER 12

Curb Appeal Magic:
Captivate Buyers from the Outside In

As you study this chapter, you may notice we've briefly discussed curb appeal in earlier chapters. Consider this chapter a renewed exploration—a deeper dive into curb appeal, its nuances, and its profound impact on the home-selling journey. Why this emphasis? Because in real estate, first impressions are not just fleeting glances; they are the lasting echoes that determine whether potential buyers will be captivated or move on.

Imagine the scene: a prospective buyer stands before two houses in the same neighborhood. Both homes boast similar square footage, layout, and amenities. However, one exudes an aura of welcoming charm, with meticulously maintained landscaping, thoughtfully placed accents, and a front door that practically beckons you inside. The other lacks the same visual allure, leaving a sense of indifference. Which home would you, as a buyer, be drawn to? The answer is clear—a home with curb appeal casts a magnetic spell, inviting exploration and igniting desire.

In the competitive real estate arena, where properties vie for attention like performers on a grand stage, presenting your home in the best possible light is not a mere suggestion; it's an imperative. As sellers, you are not just offering a structure but creating an experience. Every meticulously chosen detail, every artful touch, contributes to the narrative you wish to convey— a narrative of warmth, care, and possibility.

Why reiterate the concept of curb appeal? Because the significance of first impressions cannot be overstated. Buyers are not just purchasing a physical space; they are envisioning a future, and the journey begins with that initial glance from the curb. When potential buyers encounter a home that radiates charm, they don't merely see a house; they visualize a haven, a place to build memories, and a canvas for their dreams.

In this chapter, we delve deep into the art and science of curb appeal. We uncover the methods to transform your home's exterior into a masterpiece that captures attention, stirs emotions, and beckons buyers to explore further. From the symphony of landscaping to the psychology of color, from the subtle influence of lighting to the sensory experience of scents, we explore every facet that contributes to the enchantment of curb appeal.

Remember, you're not just competing with other homes for sale but for a potential buyer's heart and imagination. The choices you make to enhance your home's exterior are investments in that emotional connection, which can yield invaluable returns.

So, join us on this journey to unravel the magic of curb appeal to understand the nuances that make first impressions truly lasting impressions. Together, let's explore how to turn your home into an irresistible magnet, captivating buyers from the outside in, and setting the stage for a successful and lucrative home-selling endeavor.

Landscaping That Enchants: Crafting a Prelude of Beauty

Landscaping is more than just an arrangement of plants and stones; the enchanting intro sets the tone for your home's narrative. Picture this: a verdant lawn meticulously cared for, hedges trimmed with precision, and flowerbeds bursting with color—all of these elements harmoniously converging to create an ambiance that speaks volumes to potential buyers. As you peer out your window, envision a canvas of natural artistry that captures attention, evokes emotion, and beckons visitors into the embrace of your property.

A well-maintained lawn is more than just a background; it becomes a canvas that showcases the charm of your home. Your meticulous attention to nurturing your lawn reflects your commitment to every aspect of your property. Envision the sight of lush, uniformly mowed grass—an image that effortlessly radiates an aura of sophistication, professionalism, and a sense of pride in ownership.

Hedges, shaped with an artist's eye, create an elegant border that defines the contours of your property while adding a touch of sophistication. These living sculptures provide privacy and structure and impart a sense of orderliness that resonates with prospective buyers.

Flowerbeds, ablaze with nature's hues, are your opportunity to infuse life and vibrancy into your surroundings. The strategic placement of blooms, each petal chosen carefully, transforms your property into a living canvas that captures the eye and stirs the heart. The palette of colors you choose communicates different emotions—tranquility, energy, or even a touch of whimsy, inviting potential buyers to imagine themselves amidst this botanical symphony.

For those keen on filling their landscape with a personal touch, there are several DIY techniques that can enhance its allure. Here are a few to consider:

1. DIY Planting: Select and plant a variety of flowers and shrubs that thrive in your climate. Research their maintenance needs, such as watering and sunlight requirements, and create a balanced arrangement that blooms throughout the selling season.

2. Mulching Magic: Lay fresh mulch in flowerbeds and around trees. Not only does it give your landscape a polished look, but it also helps retain moisture and prevents weed growth.

3. Container Gardening: Incorporate decorative planters filled with colorful blooms. Place them strategically near entrances or pathways to add pops of color and visual interest.

4. Edging Elegance: Define the borders of your flowerbeds with edging materials such as stones, bricks, or even metal. This creates a clean separation between your lawn and garden, adding a touch of refinement.

5. Outdoor Lighting: Illuminate pathways and showcase key features with solar-powered garden lights. Soft lighting creates

an inviting ambiance and highlights your landscape's beauty during evening showings.

It's important to recognize that landscaping isn't just about aesthetics—it's an investment in the first impression your home makes. Buyers don't merely see a piece of land; they witness the manifestation of your thoughtful stewardship, the testament to the nurturing hands that have shaped this haven.

Landscaping is your opportunity to showcase the attention to detail and pride in ownership that permeates your property. As you cultivate the artistry of your outdoor spaces, remember that you're crafting an introduction to the story that your home tells. It is a story of comfort, beauty, and possibility, waiting to be explored and embraced by those who step onto your landscape.

Small Touches, Big Impact: Crafting Moments of Delight

In curb appeal, the little things often make the biggest difference. It's like sprinkling stardust—each tiny touch contributes to a magical transformation that captures the hearts of potential buyers. As you embark on this journey of enhancing your home's exterior, remember that even modest additions can yield remarkable impact. And what's the best part? These DIY touches don't have to break the bank. Let's explore a world of subtle yet significant changes that hold the power to elevate your curb appeal to new heights, even on a light budget.

1. Inviting Seating: Imagine a charming bench nestled beneath a tree or a tasteful porch swing that sways gently in the breeze. These understated additions invite prospective buyers to pause, to linger, and to imagine themselves as part of the picture. And the beauty of it is that you can often find affordable options at thrift stores, garage sales, or by repurposing existing furniture.

2. Blossoms in Abundance: Container gardens are the jewel boxes of your landscape—compact, vibrant, and bursting with life. By selecting a variety of flowering plants that thrive in your region, you can infuse color and energy into every corner of your exterior. And the cost doesn't have to be extravagant; you can opt for budget-friendly plants and DIY planters made from repurposed materials.

3. Curb Appeal in Numbers: House numbers might seem mundane, but they're like the signature of your home—a unique identifier that speaks to its personality. You can find affordable house numbers at hardware stores or online retailers. A small investment can result in a big impact.

4. The Welcoming Hue: A fresh coat of paint for the front door is like a warm embrace to those who approach your home. You don't need to buy an entire gallon; a small container of paint can often suffice for this project. Choose a hue that complements the overall aesthetic while adding a splash of character. This DIY touch can go a long way in enhancing your home's appeal.

5. Illuminating Beauty: Updated lighting fixtures enhance safety and contribute to the allure of your exterior. You can

find reasonably priced outdoor lighting options that fit your budget. Modern sconces or pendant lights can transform your entryway into a beacon of elegance, welcoming visitors day and night.

6. Inviting Accents: Plaques or signs displaying a welcoming message can infuse a personalized charm into your exterior. Many home improvement stores offer customizable plaques that can be tailored to your liking. This cost-effective addition imparts a warm and welcoming atmosphere to your home.

7. Nature's Whisper: Wind chimes or subtle water features can introduce a soothing auditory dimension to your landscape. These can often be found at garden centers or craft stores without breaking the bank. The gentle tinkling of chimes or the soft murmur of water creates a serene backdrop that complements the visual beauty of your exterior.

As you embrace these small yet impactful changes on a light budget, remember that each addition contributes to a symphony of charm, an orchestration that resonates with the hearts and aspirations of potential buyers. The goal is to create an environment that welcomes, soothes, and enchants—a space where prospective buyers can't help but envision themselves creating a lifetime of memories.

These touches stay with visitors long after they've left, igniting their imagination and kindling a connection to the home waiting to welcome them, all without straining your budget.

Staging the Exterior: Elevating Outdoor Ambiance

Staging isn't confined to the interiors of your home—it extends gracefully to the great outdoors as well. Just as a theater set is designed to captivate an audience, your exterior spaces can be staged to enchant potential buyers from the very first glance. Let's delve into the art of staging the exterior, where every corner becomes a stage for beauty and inspiration. Here are a few DIY tips that can help transform your outdoor spaces into captivating retreats:

1. Inviting Arrangements: Outdoor furniture isn't merely functional—it's an invitation to embrace the beauty of nature. Arrange your outdoor seating in an inviting manner that encourages relaxation and conversation. Create cozy nooks with chairs, sofas, and tables, allowing potential buyers to envision themselves basking in the sunlight or enjoying evenings under the stars.

2. Captivating Centerpieces: A small table adorned with a pitcher of fresh lemonade, or a vase of vibrant flowers can infuse life into your outdoor setting. These simple yet thoughtful additions paint a picture of leisurely afternoons, where sipping lemonade or sharing conversations over tea becomes a cherished ritual.

3. Reflective Elegance: Mirrors strategically placed outdoors can create an illusion of space and reflect the natural beauty of your surroundings. Vintage or repurposed mirrors can lend a touch of elegance while expanding the visual appeal of your outdoor spaces.

4. Outdoor Artistry: Hang weather-resistant artwork, sculptures, or decorative panels that complement your home's

style. These artistic elements add a unique touch to your exterior, inviting potential buyers to explore and imagine how they can personalize the space.

5. Breath of Freshness: Infuse the air with the subtle scents of nature by strategically placing potted herbs or fragrant flowers around your outdoor spaces. These natural scents can create a welcoming and refreshing ambiance that resonates with visitors.

Staging the exterior is about crafting a narrative—a story of comfort, leisure, and beauty that unfolds in every corner of your outdoor spaces. With these DIY staging tips, you invite potential buyers to see a house and envision a lifestyle that harmonizes with the surroundings. From intimate gatherings to serene moments of solitude, your staged exterior spaces portray the possibilities that await.

The Enchanting Role of Lighting: Illuminating Outdoor Allure

Outdoor lighting is a dual-purpose marvel—a functional necessity that also wields the power to elevate the aesthetic charm of your home's exterior. Thoughtfully placed lights enhance safety and visibility and weave a captivating tapestry of illumination that welcomes potential buyers even as the sun sets. Discover the magic of outdoor lighting and how a few DIY touches can transform your property into a captivating oasis. Here are some budget-friendly DIY tips to infuse your outdoor spaces with enchanting illumination:

Solar-Powered Splendor: Solar lights are a budget-friendly and eco-conscious option to add a touch of ethereal glow to your property. They harness the power of the sun during the day, casting a gentle radiance throughout the night. You can find a variety of solar night lights in the market, ranging from $1 to $10, depending on the store you shop at. These lights come in various designs and sizes, making it easy to find ones that complement your outdoor aesthetic.

Guiding Pathways: Illuminate pathways and walkways leading to your home with strategically placed lights. Solar path lights can be inserted directly into the ground or secured along the edges of your pathways. Doing this adds an inviting glow to your home and ensures safety for potential buyers during evening showings.

Accentuating Architecture: Showcase the architectural features of your home by using lighting to accentuate its unique elements; position lights to highlight intricate designs, columns, or entryways. This draws attention to the exquisite craftsmanship of your home, even in the evening hours.

Landscape Illumination: Illuminate your landscaping elements to create a multi-dimensional allure. Consider installing spotlights to showcase ornamental trees, shrubs, or flower beds. Soft lighting can enhance the beauty of your garden, adding layers of depth and texture to the surroundings.

Dramatic Backdrops: Add string lights to enhance the appeal of outdoor seating areas, decks, or patios. These charming lights can be draped along railings, strung between poles, or suspended above seating areas, creating a captivating atmosphere for evening gatherings.

Moonlit Reflections: If you have a water feature like a pond or fountain, consider adding underwater or floating lights. These lights cast shimmering reflections on the water's surface, evoking a serene and enchanting ambiance that captivates the senses.

Garden Delights: Elevate your garden's allure by wrapping solar string lights around tree trunks or trellises. These lights create a whimsical and magical atmosphere that beckons visitors to explore the outdoor wonderland you've created.

Economical Elegance: For a pocket-friendly approach, use mason jars or glass containers to house tea lights or flameless candles. Place them along garden paths, on outdoor tables, or hang them from trees to infuse a warm and inviting glow.

Radiant Entryways: Illuminate your front porch or entryway with stylish wall-mounted lights or pendant fixtures. These additions provide essential lighting and contribute to the curb appeal, leaving a lasting impression on potential buyers.

Custom Illumination: DIY enthusiasts can craft unique lighting fixtures using repurposed materials. Upcycle vintage lanterns, create your own pendant lights, or design a chandelier from items you already have on hand. This adds a personal touch and a dash of creativity to your outdoor lighting design.

By harnessing the captivating power of lighting, you're transforming your outdoor spaces into a symphony of radiance. From the gentle glow of solar lights to the artistic allure of custom fixtures, your property gains a distinct identity as the sun dips below the horizon. And remember, it's not just about showcasing the home—it's about igniting the imagination of potential buyers, allowing them to envision the luminous life that could be theirs.

Invoking Emotion Through Color

Color is a powerful tool that can stir emotions and establish distinct moods. As you set out to select colors for your home's exterior, recognize the profound impact they can have on potential buyers. Beyond mere aesthetics, colors resonate deeply with individuals, triggering feelings that influence their perception of your property. Therefore, it's essential to deliberate on the emotions you intend to evoke and the atmosphere you aim to create within the minds of those who approach your home.

Consider the personality and character you wish to infuse when selecting colors for your home's exterior space. Earthy tones, such as warm browns and serene greens, have the uncanny ability to generate feelings of comfort and intimacy. These colors can wrap your home in a sense of tranquility, making it appear inviting and harmonious.

On the other hand, vibrant and bold hues can inject your home with a burst of energy and liveliness. Reds, yellows, and blues can awaken the senses and create an atmosphere of dynamism. These colors project confidence and vitality, potentially catching the eye of passersby and sparking their curiosity.

It's worth noting that you don't necessarily have to paint the entire house; simple touch-ups can work wonders. A fresh coat of paint on the front door or window trims can bring a renewed vibrancy to the exterior. These touch-ups, even in carefully chosen colors, can make a significant impact.

Moreover, consider the environment in which your home is situated. The natural landscape and surroundings can play a role in the color choices that harmonize best with the outdoor setting. For instance, a home nestled within a lush green environment might benefit from earthy tones that seamlessly blend with nature, while a house located near the coast could find inspiration in the soft blues and sandy beiges of the sea and shore.

As you ponder your color choices, remember that the goal is to enhance your home's curb appeal and conjure a visceral response within potential buyers. The right colors can resonate with them on a subconscious level, shaping their perception of your property even before they step foot inside. By thoughtfully considering the emotions you wish to evoke and selecting colors that resonate with your vision, you can harness the power of color to captivate and connect with prospective buyers.

The Curb Appeal Advantage

Time, effort, and resources are investments that will enhance your home's curb appeal and have the potential to yield substantial returns. Not only does it draw buyers in, but it also contributes to a higher perceived value. A property with an enchanting exterior invites curiosity and enthusiasm, increasing the likelihood of a successful sale.

From meticulously maintained landscaping to thoughtfully chosen exterior décor, the magic of curb appeal encapsulates a blend of art and strategy. With each glance from potential buyers, your home's exterior tells a story of care, attention, and possibility. This chapter peels back the layers of curb appeal, revealing how this enchanting element can turn mere curiosity into fervent interest and, ultimately, transform viewers into eager buyers.

CHAPTER 13

The Art of Effective Home Marketing: Reaching Your Ideal Audience

Effective marketing is the cornerstone of a successful sale. Just as a skilled storyteller tailor their narrative to captivate a specific audience, home sellers must strategically craft their marketing approach to resonate with the right potential buyers. This chapter delves into the techniques of home marketing, focusing on reaching your ideal audience and making your home stand out in a competitive market.

Understanding Your Target Audience: The First Step

Before diving into the world of home marketing, it's essential to understand your target audience intimately. Each property has its unique appeal, catering to specific groups of buyers. Whether your home is perfect for families, urban professionals, or retirees, identifying the demographics, preferences, and aspirations of your potential buyers lays the foundation for successful marketing.

Showcasing Your Home's Unique Story: Visual Impact

In today's digital age, visual storytelling is paramount. Engaging visuals play a pivotal role in capturing initial interest in online listings. Collaborating with a professional photographer to capture your home's essence—the nuanced details, interplay of light, and inviting spaces—can set it apart. Consider creating a virtual tour to provide potential buyers with an immersive experience of your property. This tool allows them to explore the layout and flow of your home remotely. Staging your property for these visuals enhances their impact, enabling potential buyers to envision themselves living there.

The Digital Arena: Leveraging Online Platforms

The digital realm offers a vast landscape for showcasing your home's virtues. Utilize multiple online platforms to amplify your reach and engage a wider audience. Listing your home on reputable real estate websites, like the Multiple Listing Service (MLS), ensures it gains exposure to agents and buyers alike.

Social media platforms provide another potent tool. Utilize captivating images, engaging captions, and relevant hashtags to draw attention to your listing. Posts showcasing unique features, nearby attractions, and the lifestyle your home offers can generate interest and shares.

Traditional and Digital Synergy: A Comprehensive Approach

Effective home marketing requires a harmonious blend of traditional and digital efforts. While online platforms are critical, traditional methods should not be overlooked. Print ads, postcards, and flyers have their place in drawing people's attention. Online ads through Google and social media platforms like Facebook can significantly extend your property's reach to targeted audiences.

Expert Assistance: Collaborating with Real Estate Professionals

Though DIY marketing can be effective, engaging real estate professionals can enhance your efforts. An experienced agent brings insights into market trends, buyer preferences, and effective marketing strategies. They craft a compelling narrative that resonates with your target audience, ensuring your property stands out.

Open Houses and Private Showings: Elevating the Experience

In-person viewings are pivotal in the marketing journey. Open houses and private showings offer prospects the chance to experience your home firsthand. Ensure your space is immaculate, well-staged, and inviting. Create an environment where visitors can seamlessly imagine themselves living there.

Leaving a Lasting Impression

Effective home marketing extends beyond the transaction. Provide potential buyers with informative brochures or digital materials highlighting your home's attributes, neighborhood amenities, and local attractions. This thoughtful gesture helps your property remain in their minds as they continue their home search.

In conclusion, the art of effective home marketing weaves together your property's unique features with the aspirations of your target audience. By comprehending your buyers, crafting compelling visuals, utilizing both traditional and digital platforms, and leveraging expert guidance, you ensure your home's story reaches those most likely to embrace it as their own.

CHAPTER 14

Common Mistakes to Avoid: Pitfalls That Can Cost You

In the intricate realm of real estate, success often hinges on avoiding common pitfalls that can inadvertently sabotage your efforts. These missteps, though seemingly innocuous, can have far-reaching consequences that impact your selling experience and final outcome. By recognizing these pitfalls and understanding how to sidestep them, you can navigate the selling process with greater confidence and avoid unnecessary setbacks.

Overpricing: The Price Paradox

One of the most prevalent mistakes sellers make is overpricing their home. While you might believe that setting a higher price leaves room for negotiation, it often has the opposite effect. Overpriced homes tend to linger on the market, deterring potential buyers who perceive them as unattainable or inflated. Avoid this pitfall by conducting thorough market research and working closely with your real estate agent to determine a competitive and realistic price that reflects your property's value.

Neglecting Repairs and Upgrades

Failing to address necessary repairs and upgrades can

significantly diminish your home's appeal. Buyers are more likely to be drawn to properties that are move-in ready, and the presence of visible issues can raise concerns and result in lower offers. Prioritize repairs such as leaky faucets, chipped paint, and broken fixtures. Additionally, consider modest upgrades that can add value, such as fresh paint, updated lighting, or new hardware.

Inadequate Staging: Underestimating Visual Impact

Underestimating the power of staging is a pitfall that can hinder your selling efforts. A well-staged home allows potential buyers to envision themselves living in the space and creates a sense of emotional connection. Avoid this mistake by decluttering, depersonalizing, and strategically arranging furniture and décor to highlight your home's best features. If necessary, consider seeking professional staging services to optimize visual appeal.

Poor Photography: Capturing the Essence

In the digital age, the importance of high-quality photography cannot be overstated. Grainy or poorly lit photos can undermine your marketing efforts and deter potential buyers from scheduling viewings. Avoid this pitfall by enlisting a professional photographer who can capture your home's essence and showcase it in the best light. These images are often a buyer's first impression, so investing in good photography is essential.

Neglecting Curb Appeal: A Missed Opportunity

Curb appeal sets the tone for a buyer's perception of your home. Neglecting the exterior can create a lackluster first impression that impacts their overall impression. Avoid this pitfall by enhancing your home's curb appeal through landscaping, a well-maintained exterior, and minor exterior upgrades. Remember, the exterior is the first thing buyers see, so a little effort can go a long way in creating a positive impression.

Inflexibility with Showings: Missed Opportunities

Being inflexible with showing appointments can limit the number of potential buyers who view your home. While accommodating showings can be inconvenient, it's essential to maximize exposure to interested parties. Avoid this pitfall by keeping your home in showing condition and being open to flexible showing times. The more accessible your home is to potential buyers, the higher your chances of a successful sale.

Ignoring Market Trends: A Disconnect with Reality

Market trends play a significant role in determining your home's value and desirability. Ignoring these trends can result in unrealistic pricing or poor marketing strategies. Avoid this pitfall by staying informed about current market conditions, working closely with your real estate agent, and being willing to adjust your approach based on changing trends.

Pitfalls to Avoid When Selling a Tenant-Occupied Home:

Selling a home that tenants currently occupy can present unique challenges, and avoiding common pitfalls is crucial to ensure a smooth and successful sale. One of the most significant mistakes a seller can make in this scenario is failing to communicate with the tenants promptly. Often, sellers don't inform their tenants about the decision to sell the property, which can lead to confusion and discomfort. It's essential to maintain transparency and have an open conversation with the tenants, explaining the situation and the steps that will be taken.

Another common misstep is underestimating the impact of the sale on the tenants. The uncertainty of a new owner or the fear of eviction can create anxiety among tenants, potentially leading to a less-than-ideal living situation. Sellers should consider the emotional aspect of the tenants during this process and take measures to minimize their discomfort. This might involve offering incentives for cooperation or negotiating with the tenants to assist them in relocating.

Furthermore, sellers should be aware of the legal implications involved in selling a tenant-occupied property. Failure to adhere to local rental laws and regulations can lead to delays and legal issues that can be costly. It's essential to consult with legal counsel and leverage the expertise of a real estate professional experienced in navigating sensitive complexities effectively.

Disregarding Agent Expertise: A Missed Resource

Disregarding the expertise of your real estate agent is a common mistake that can hinder your selling process. Your agent brings valuable insights into the market, pricing strategies, and negotiation techniques. Avoid this pitfall by actively engaging with your agent, seeking their advice, and collaborating closely to make informed decisions that align with your goals.

In conclusion, understanding and avoiding these common pitfalls can greatly enhance your home selling experience. By setting a competitive price, addressing repairs and upgrades, staging effectively, investing in quality photography, prioritizing curb appeal, remaining flexible with showings, staying informed about market trends, and valuing your agent's expertise, you can navigate the selling process with confidence and increase your chances of a successful sale.

CHAPTER 15

Unlocking the Buyer's Mind: Strategies for Finding Your Perfect Buyer

The journey of selling a home is not solely about presenting a property; it's also about understanding the desires, preferences, and motivations of potential buyers. Successfully unlocking the buyer's mind requires a strategic approach that goes beyond the physical aspects of your home. This chapter delves into the art of comprehending buyer psychology, equipping you with the strategies necessary to attract and engage the perfect buyer for your property.

Understanding Buyer Personas: The Blueprint for Connection

Buyers are as diverse as the homes they seek. Crafting buyer personas—a detailed representation of your ideal buyers— provides invaluable insights into their lifestyles, aspirations, and priorities. These personas guide your marketing efforts, enabling you to tailor your messaging to resonate with specific segments of the buyer market.

Begin by analyzing the features of your home and its location. Does your property cater to families seeking spacious living spaces and proximity to schools? Is it a haven for urban professionals drawn to modern amenities and a vibrant city life? Understanding these nuances helps you create compelling narratives that appeal to the emotions and lifestyles of different buyer personas.

Mastering Emotional Connection: The Heart of the Sale

Emotions play a significant role in the home-buying process. Buyers seek homes that resonate with their aspirations and evoke positive feelings. To unlock the buyer's mind:

1. Focus on the emotional journey your property can offer.
2. Craft your marketing materials to showcase the experiences and memories that living in your home can provide.
3. Highlight the moments that prospective buyers can envision sharing with their loved ones, whether it's cozy evenings by the fireplace, joyful gatherings in the backyard, or tranquil mornings on the porch.

Telling Your Home's Story: A Narrative of Possibilities

Every home has a story to tell, a narrative of the life it has hosted and the dreams it has inspired. Infuse your marketing efforts with this narrative, capturing the essence of your home's history and the potential it holds for future owners. Use compelling language to describe the unique features, architectural details, and distinctive charm that set your property apart. Paint a vivid picture that allows potential buyers to visualize themselves as the protagonists of this story.

Effective Home Staging: Inviting Possibilities

Staging your home strategically can unlock the buyer's imagination and help them envision the lifestyle it offers. Create settings that illustrate the versatility and functionality of different spaces. Transform an extra bedroom into a cozy home office, a nook into a reading corner, or an outdoor area into an al fresco dining retreat. By staging with purpose, you empower buyers to see the potential for their own lives within your home.

Curating Virtual Experiences: Embracing Technology

In a digitally driven world, virtual experiences play a pivotal role in unlocking the buyer's mind. Utilize virtual tours, 3D walkthroughs, and interactive floor plans to provide an immersive experience that transcends physical barriers. These technologies allow potential buyers to explore your home at their convenience, enhancing their emotional connection and enabling them to envision themselves as part of the space.

The Power of Presentation: Highlighting Unique Features

Each home possesses distinctive features that can profoundly appeal to the perfect buyer. Whether it's an enchanting bay window, a meticulously crafted fireplace, or a beautifully landscaped backyard, these attributes can be the catalyst for capturing the buyer's attention. Present these characteristics in your marketing materials and conversations with prospective buyers. Emphasize how these features enhance the overall lifestyle that your home provides.

Engaging in Authentic Conversations: Listening and Responding

Unlocking the buyer's mind is also about engaging in authentic conversations. Listen attentively to potential buyers' questions, concerns, and preferences. Address their inquiries transparently and provide information that aligns with their needs. Authenticity fosters trust and builds a strong connection that can lead to a successful transaction.

Building a Sense of Urgency: Encouraging Action

Instilling a sense of urgency can incentivize prospective buyers to act promptly. Strategies like limited-time offers or showcasing the demand for your property can unlock the buyer's mind by prompting them to act swiftly. However, it's essential to strike a balance between urgency and pressure, ensuring that buyers feel empowered to make informed decisions.

Cultivating a Lasting Impression: Beyond the Sale

Unlocking the buyer's mind extends beyond the moment of sale. Leave a lasting impression by providing personalized information about the neighborhood, nearby amenities, and local attractions. This gesture not only enhances the buying experience but also fosters a positive connection that can lead to referrals and positive reviews.

In the end, unlocking the buyer's mind requires a holistic approach that merges understanding, emotional connection, technology, and authentic engagement. By crafting compelling narratives, staging effectively, embracing virtual experiences, highlighting unique features, engaging in meaningful conversations, and creating a sense of urgency, you can unlock the buyer's imagination and help them see the endless possibilities your home holds.

CHAPTER 16

Mastering the Art of Win-Win: Navigating Successful Negotiations

Negotiations hold the key to achieving a win-win outcome. The art of negotiation is not only about price; it encompasses a harmonious balance between the seller's goals and the buyer's aspirations. This chapter delves into the strategies and approaches that guide you through successful negotiations, fostering a positive and mutually beneficial experience for all parties involved.

The Foundations of Win-Win Negotiations

At the heart of successful negotiations lies the principle of win-win—a scenario where both parties emerge satisfied with the terms of the agreement. To achieve this, approach negotiations with an open mind and a willingness to find common ground. Understand that flexibility is a valuable asset; while your ideal outcome is essential, consider various possibilities that could meet both your objectives and the buyer's desires.

The Art of Compromise and Flexibility

Negotiations often involve a give-and-take process. While your listing price sets the stage, be prepared to adjust based on market conditions and buyer feedback. Offering buyer credits, contributing to closing costs, or even allowing potential buyers to experience the home by staying for a weekend can demonstrate your flexibility and genuine interest in accommodating their needs.

Flexibility extends beyond price adjustments. For instance, consider including a home warranty as part of the deal. This gesture provides buyers with peace of mind, knowing that if unexpected repairs arise, they have a safety net. Such acts can resonate with buyers, enhancing the perceived value of your home and fostering a sense of trust.

Navigating Counteroffers and Collaborative Discussions

Counteroffers are a natural part of negotiations. Respond to counteroffers thoughtfully and considerately. Acknowledge the buyer's position and provide clear rationale for your counterproposal. Maintain open lines of communication, discussing terms with transparency and respect. Collaborative discussions can lead to creative solutions, bridging the gap between your positions.

Leveraging Professional Representation: Your Real Estate Agent

Your real estate agent plays a pivotal role in negotiations. Drawing from their expertise, they can guide you through the process, offering insights into market trends, buyer preferences, and negotiation strategies. They act as intermediaries, facilitating constructive discussions while safeguarding your interests. Their objective perspective can help you make informed decisions that lead to successful outcomes.

The Power of Perspective: Seeing Beyond the Transaction

Negotiations should not be viewed as isolated events; they're part of a broader journey towards a successful sale. Consider the bigger picture, taking into account the value of fostering positive relationships. A successful negotiation sets the tone for a smooth transaction and can lead to referrals and positive reviews. Building rapport and maintaining professionalism contribute to an overall positive experience.

Navigating the Terrain of Win-Win

Mastering the art of win-win negotiations requires a balanced approach that values both your goals as a seller and the aspirations of potential buyers. An open mind, flexibility, and the willingness to explore various solutions can lead to a harmonious agreement. You can navigate negotiations with confidence and grace by offering compromises, considering buyer preferences, and collaborating with your real estate agent.

In the end, successful negotiations transcend monetary transactions; they reflect a harmonious alignment of goals and values. By embracing the principles of win-win, you not only achieve your desired outcome but also contribute to an atmosphere of mutual respect and satisfaction that echoes long after the ink on the contract has dried.

CHAPTER 17

Navigating Legal Aspects: Ensuring a Smooth Sale Process

This chapter delves into the legal considerations that underpin a successful sale, offering insights into seller responsibilities, various listing agreements, and the importance of an exclusive listing agreement. Moreover, we explore the significance of addressing title issues, taxes, liens, and potential encumbrances, ensuring a clear path toward a secure and uncomplicated transaction.

Understanding Seller Responsibilities: The Listing Agreement

When initiating the sale of your home, a pivotal step involves signing a listing agreement. This contractual document formalizes your partnership with a real estate agent, establishing essential parameters for the sale. Within this agreement, critical details are outlined, encompassing the property's asking price, the agent's commission, the listing duration, and the extent of anything you want to exclude from the sale. By signing this agreement, you bestow upon your chosen agent the authority to represent your interests, manage the marketing of your property, and skillfully negotiate on your behalf.

In this chapter we will discuss two types of listing agreements: An exclusive right-to-sell agency listing agreement, the seller agrees to work exclusively with one real estate agent or brokerage. This agreement has the highest level of commitment to the seller because it holds the agent and brokerage to a high standard of confidentiality and fiduciary duty. This arrangement often provides access to premium agent services, such as seller deferred renovation programs, professional staging, and comprehensive marketing strategies. These added advantages can significantly enhance the overall effectiveness of your home sale, ensuring that your property is presented in the best possible light and reaches its full market potential.

On the other hand, in a limited agency listing agreement, the seller is open to work with whomever procures a buyer. This type of agreement is also known as an open agency agreement, although it's worth noting that agents rarely agree to offer it due to the limited protection it provides to the seller and brokerage.

Clearing the Path: Addressing Title Issues and Liens

One of the pivotal legal considerations in a real estate transaction is the property's title. Title issues, such as encumbrances, liens, or competing claims, can cloud the ownership of a property and impede a sale. Before listing your home, it's important to complete a title search to identify any potential liens, judgments, or unexpected ownership changes. Addressing these issues proactively can prevent last-minute disruptions and convey a clear title to the buyer.

Clouded Title: Navigating Potential Encumbrances

An encumbrance is a claim or liability that affects the ownership of a property. Common encumbrances include mortgages, property taxes, and easements. Clearing these encumbrances ensures that your property is free from legal entanglements that could deter potential buyers. By addressing these matters upfront, you instill confidence in your property's legal standing and facilitate a smoother transaction process.

The Role of Property Taxes in Real Estate Transactions

Property taxes are a fundamental aspect of homeownership and real estate transactions. These local taxes are levied on real property, which typically includes land and any structures on it. They serve as a vital source of revenue for financing essential public services like schools, public safety, infrastructure maintenance, and more within specific jurisdictions, often cities or counties.

Property taxes come into play in various ways when selling a home:

Firstly, property taxes are the responsibility of the property owner. Homeowners are required to pay property taxes regularly, usually on an annual or semi-annual basis, to their local taxing authority. The amount owed depends on the assessed value of the property and the tax rate set by the local government. Importantly, the assessed value may differ from the property's market value.

Sellers are often legally required to disclose information about the property's current property tax status when selling a home. This includes details about the property's assessed value, any outstanding property tax amounts, and information on upcoming tax assessments or changes in tax rates that might affect the buyer.

Property owners also have the right to appeal their property tax assessments if they believe the assessed value is too high. Additionally, certain exemptions or deductions may be available for specific property owners, such as senior citizens or veterans, which can reduce their property tax liability.

In summary, it's important to know the status of your property taxes and ensure they are paid timely. If a homeowner's property taxes are not paid up to date, they can expect to pay the balance through escrow prior to transferring ownership to the new buyer.

The Role of Legal Professionals: Navigating Complexity

Enlisting the services of an experienced qualified real estate attorney can be invaluable, especially when dealing with legal complexities. Attorneys can review contracts, ensure compliance with local laws, and provide guidance on navigating intricate legal matters. Their expertise adds an extra layer of protection, mitigating potential risks and fostering a secure and seamless sale process.

The Path Forward: A Legally Sound Journey

Legal considerations compose a crucial movement in the symphony of real estate transactions. You chart a path towards a successful sale by understanding your responsibilities as a seller, choosing the right listing agreement, and proactively addressing issues to avoid delays in your sale. Navigating the legal landscape requires diligence and a commitment to transparency. By adhering to these principles and being well-informed, you pave the way for a transaction that not only satisfies legal requirements but also nurtures a sense of security and trust for all parties involved.

CHAPTER 18

Strategic Financial Decisions: Maximizing ROI for Sellers

Your financial choices form the bedrock of your return on investment (ROI). This chapter delves into the realm of strategic financial planning for sellers, exploring the vital considerations that guide you toward astute decisions, ultimately optimizing your property's financial potential. By intertwining pricing strategies, cost management, tax implications, and the art of concessions, you can adeptly navigate the complex landscape to secure the highest returns for your property.

Pricing Strategies: The Balancing Act of Valuation

Setting the optimal price for your property involves a delicate equilibrium between value and market dynamics. Collaborating with your real estate agent, who deeply understands the local market, ensures a nuanced pricing strategy. Overpricing can deter potential buyers while underpricing might lead to missed opportunities. A meticulous analysis of comparable sales and your property's unique features guides you toward a balanced price that resonates with the market.

Cost Management: Enhancing Value through Investment

One of the pivotal ways to boost your ROI is through prudent investments aimed at enhancing your property's appeal. As you consider potential upgrades, focus on those that yield significant returns. Kitchen and bathroom improvements, for instance, often provide substantial value by enhancing the functionality and aesthetics of these key areas.

Curb appeal enhancements play a critical role as well. The exterior of your home is the first thing potential buyers see, and a well-maintained and inviting façade can set a positive tone for their perception of the entire property. This might involve tasks like landscaping, repairing any visible wear and tear, and perhaps even repainting the front door or shutters.

Strategic decluttering is a cost-effective investment. Eliminating personal items and simplifying the decor can aid potential buyers in picturing themselves residing in the home. It establishes a neutral backdrop that enables them to mentally envision the property as their own.

Recognizing the threshold at which your investments yield diminishing returns is essential. Over-investing in your property beyond the norms of your neighborhood might not necessarily translate into higher returns. Understanding the local real estate market and its expectations is crucial here. Your real estate agent can offer valuable insights regarding the upgrades that appeal most to buyers in your locality.

However, it's not just major renovations that make a difference. Smaller investments can also have a significant impact. Applying a fresh coat of paint can rejuvenate a room, while addressing minor repairs can eliminate potential concerns that might deter buyers. Staging your home with carefully chosen furniture and décor can help potential buyers see the space's full potential.

Tax Implications: Navigating the Financial Landscape

Understanding the intricacies of tax implications is vital in strategic decision-making. Capital gains tax can considerably impact your financial returns. Consulting a tax professional to explore options like the 1031 exchange can help defer capital gains tax by reinvesting in another property. This knowledge empowers you to make choices aligned with your long-term financial goals.

Concessions: Fine-Tuning the Negotiation

Seller concessions can be instrumental in attracting buyers, yet they impact your net gain. These concessions often involve assisting buyers with costs related to the purchase, such as covering part of the closing costs, repairs, or home warranties. While concessions can sweeten the deal and make your property more appealing, it's essential to approach them with strategic finesse.

Carefully evaluate local market conditions to gauge the competitiveness of your offering. Consider the preferences and motivations of potential buyers. Are they first-time homebuyers looking to minimize upfront costs? Are they looking for move-in-ready properties or those with room for improvement? Tailoring your concessions to align with these factors can give you a competitive edge.

Moreover, assessing your financial goals is pivotal. Determine the maximum concessions you can provide without jeopardizing your desired ROI. Collaborating closely with your real estate agent is crucial during this phase. They can provide insights into buyer expectations, local market trends, and potential concessions that can effectively sway negotiations in your favor.

Striking a balance is key—offer concessions that add value for buyers without significantly compromising your overall returns. For instance, covering a portion of closing costs or providing a home warranty can be attractive incentives without eroding your financial gains. You can effectively navigate negotiations and cultivate a mutually beneficial outcome for both parties by fine-tuning your concession strategy.

Financial Timing: Capitalizing on Market Trends

Timing is a pivotal factor in the world of real estate. Collaborating with your agent to identify favorable market windows can lead to more profitable outcomes. Selling during peak seasons or heightened buyer demand enhances your chances of a favorable ROI.

Leveraging ROI: Opportunities on the Horizon

The culmination of a successful sale opens the door to a myriad of financial prospects, each offering the potential to shape your future in distinct ways. The proceeds from your sale represent more than just a monetary sum; they are the catalyst for achieving your aspirations and securing your financial well-being. This section delves into the array of opportunities that await you after the sale, guiding you toward informed decisions that align with your unique goals.

1. Securing Your Future: Building Retirement Savings

Planning for retirement is an integral aspect of financial stewardship. The funds from selling your property can substantially enhance your retirement nest egg. By designating a share of these proceeds to go into a retirement fund like a 401(k), Individual Retirement Account (IRA), or a life insurance policy can be a prudent choice to secure your financial well-being in the years ahead. These funds can grow over time, ensuring your golden years are characterized by financial comfort and independence.

2. Portfolio Diversification: Investing in Your Financial Growth

The path to financial prosperity often involves diversifying your investment portfolio. Real estate can continue to play a pivotal role in this strategy. Consider reinvesting a portion of your proceeds in another property that aligns with your investment goals. This could be a rental property that generates passive income, a vacation home that doubles as an investment and a retreat, or a property in a growing market that promises substantial appreciation over time. Diversifying your investments mitigates risks and positions you to capitalize on various market trends.

3. Upgrading for Growth: Enhancing Your Living Space

If your family is expanding or your needs are evolving, the proceeds from your sale can facilitate a seamless transition. Upsizing to a larger property can provide the space and amenities necessary to accommodate your family's growth and changing lifestyle. Whether it's a larger backyard, more bedrooms, or upgraded features, the opportunity to enhance your living space is within reach. This decision blends practicality with investment potential, as well-maintained and thoughtfully upgraded homes tend to appreciate in value.

4. Embracing Financial Freedom: Downsizing Strategically

Downsizing offers a unique avenue to optimize your financial freedom. If your current property exceeds your needs, selling and downsizing to a more manageable space can unlock substantial equity. The surplus funds can be allocated to various financial goals, from bolstering your retirement savings to embarking on new adventures. Downsizing can also lead to reduced maintenance and utility costs, allowing you to enjoy life with fewer financial burdens.

5. Funding Life's Enjoyments: Embarking on New Adventures

Perhaps the first vision that comes to mind is using the proceeds to fund a long-awaited vacation—a well-deserved reward for the effort invested in the sale process. Whether it's an exotic getaway, a cruise to uncharted waters, or an exploration of cultural landscapes, the infusion of funds from your sale can transform dreams into reality. This is an opportunity to create cherished memories with loved ones and immerse yourself in experiences that rejuvenate the spirit.

Making Informed Choices: Evaluating Your Options

The key to harnessing the potential of your proceeds lies in making informed decisions that align with your aspirations and financial goals. Reflect on what matters most to you—whether it's financial security, growth, experiences, or a combination of these factors. Consult financial advisors who can help you evaluate the tax implications, investment potential, and long-term implications of each option.

Ultimately, the proceeds from your property sale are a canvas of opportunity waiting for you to paint your financial masterpiece. Each decision you make is a brushstroke that shapes your future, and the choices you craft today can reverberate for years to come. Whether you're investing, upgrading, downsizing, or embarking on new adventures, the potential for financial success is at your fingertips. Your property sale isn't just an endpoint; it's the beginning of a new chapter filled with possibilities.

Expert Guidance: Collaborating with Professionals

The role of expert guidance cannot be overstated. The landscape is rich with possibilities but also fraught with complexities that require astute navigation. Collaborating with seasoned professionals ensures that your choices are well-informed, strategic, and tailored to your unique circumstances. This section delves deeper into the importance of seeking expert advice and the key professionals to engage for a well-rounded approach.

1. Financial Advisors: Crafting a Comprehensive Strategy

Financial advisors act as the designers of your financial future. They bring a profound comprehension of investment options, risk mitigation, and the intricacies of long-term financial strategizing. With their expertise, they evaluate your financial objectives, capacity for risk, and overall financial portfolio to craft a holistic plan that harmonizes with your ambitions.

Whether you're considering investing in another property, saving for retirement, or pursuing other ventures, a financial advisor can help you make choices that harmonize with your broader financial landscape.

2. Tax Professionals: Navigating Tax Implications

The tax implications of your financial decisions are a crucial consideration. A tax professional can provide insights into how various options impact your tax liability. For instance, selling a property can have capital gains tax implications, while investing in certain assets may offer tax advantages. By collaborating with a tax expert, you can explore strategies that minimize tax burdens, optimize deductions, and ensure compliance with tax regulations.

3. Real Estate Experts: Gaining Market Insights

Engaging with a real estate expert can be invaluable if you consider reinvesting in real estate. These professionals deeply understand market trends, property valuations, and investment potential. They can help you identify properties that align with your investment goals, evaluate their potential for appreciation, and navigate the complexities of property transactions. Whether you're exploring rental properties, vacation homes, or other real estate ventures, a real estate expert can provide critical insights to guide your decisions.

4. Legal Professionals: Ensuring Compliance and Protection

Financial decisions like investing in real estate or setting up a trust may involve legal complexities. Legal professionals, such as real estate attorneys or estate planners, can provide guidance to ensure compliance with regulations and protection of your interests. They can draft contracts, review agreements, and provide advice on structuring transactions that align with your goals while safeguarding your legal rights.

Crafting Your Financial Roadmap: The Collaborative Approach

The convergence of financial considerations after a successful property sale requires a collaborative approach. Engaging with financial advisors, tax professionals, real estate experts, and legal advisors lets you view your financial canvas from multiple angles. When harmonized, these professionals bring diverse expertise that results in a comprehensive and strategic roadmap for your post-sale journey.

As you evaluate your options—whether investing in real estate, planning for retirement, or embarking on new adventures—remember that expert guidance empowers you to make informed choices. The synergy of professional insights, aligned with your aspirations, positions you to harness the potential of your proceeds in ways that amplify their impact. Your financial decisions are a mosaic of opportunity, and the collaborative approach ensures that each piece contributes to the masterpiece of your financial success.

Conclusion: Crafting Financial Success

In the intricate web of real estate transactions and the complexities of financial decision-making, the pursuit of maximizing ROI emerges as a comprehensive and deliberate journey. As you navigate this path, it becomes evident that each choice is a brushstroke contributing to the masterpiece of your financial success. This chapter has delved deep into strategic financial decisions, offering insights that illuminate the nuances of pricing, investing, and leveraging opportunities.

Maximizing ROI involves a sequence of calculated steps, from carefully evaluating your property's value to enhancing its presentation. This process demands a thoughtful approach, where your decisions are influenced by your short-term objectives and long-term financial aspirations. The fabric of financial success is crafted through a combination of foresight, strategic planning, and collaborative efforts.

The expertise of financial advisors, tax experts, real estate professionals, and legal advisors adds depth and perspective to your financial canvas. When harmonized with your goals, their insights lead to a symphony of choices that resonate with your unique circumstances. This collaborative approach ensures that your financial roadmap is comprehensive, balanced, and poised for success.

As you progress into the post-sale phase, remember that your decisions reverberate through time, impacting your future in visible and concealed ways. The financial choices you make today hold the power to shape tomorrow's landscape. Each investment and every strategic move contributes to the narrative of your financial story. The home you've sold is not merely a structure—it's a vessel of possibility, a cornerstone of potential that propels you toward realizing your dreams.

In the grand orchestration of financial success, your vision takes center stage. Your aspirations guide the composition, and your choices breathe life into the symphony of opportunity. By embracing the insights shared within this chapter, you are poised to navigate the complexities of financial decision-making with confidence and clarity. May your journey be marked by calculated steps, resonant choices, and the realization of your goals. As this chapter concludes, a new chapter begins—one where your financial success takes its rightful place in the spotlight.

CHAPTER 19

Streamline Closing: Efficiently Finalizing the Sale

As you stand on the threshold of concluding your real estate journey, the process of closing the sale emerges as the final and crucial step. This chapter is dedicated to unraveling the intricacies of streamlining the closing process, ensuring a seamless transition from negotiations to the finalization of the sale. You can navigate this pivotal phase confidently and efficiently through meticulous preparation, clear communication, and a collaborative approach.

Preparing for the Final Stretch: Assembling the Puzzle

Finalizing the sale is comparable to piecing together a puzzle, where each element contributes to forming the complete picture. During this phase, the focus shifts towards the paperwork and legal procedures. Your real estate agent, alongside a team of experts, is dedicated to meticulously preparing and organizing all necessary documents. This encompasses the purchase agreement, title records, loan particulars, and any obligatory disclosures mandated by legal regulations.

As the seller, your responsibility includes gathering essential information, such as property tax records, utility bills, and any warranties or manuals for appliances that will be handed over to the new owner. Collaborating closely with your agent and legal advisors ensures no critical detail is overlooked, minimizing potential hiccups during the closing process.

Title Matters: Ensuring a Clean Transfer

A crucial aspect of closing the sale involves ensuring a clean transfer of title. This means addressing title issues or liens that could cloud the property's ownership rights. Conducting a thorough title search helps uncover any potential obstacles that might affect the transfer of ownership. If any issues arise, they must be resolved before the closing date to ensure a smooth transition.

Title insurance is another protective measure that provides financial coverage in case any unforeseen title issues surface after the sale is finalized. While it's an additional cost, it offers peace of mind and safeguards both the buyer and seller against potential legal complications.

Repairs and Final Walkthrough

Before the closing date, the buyer typically conducts a final property walkthrough. This allows them to ensure that any agreed-upon repairs have been completed and that the property is in the expected condition. As the seller, ensuring that the property is in the agreed-upon condition for this walkthrough is essential.

Navigating Escrow and Financial Steps

The closing process involves several financial steps that contribute to the successful transfer of ownership. The buyer's lender typically requests an appraisal to ensure the purchase price aligns with the property's value. After the appraisal is finished, the buyer's lender will proceed to compile the required documents for the closing.

The remaining balance from the buyer is deposited with the title company, and funds are transferred to your bank account as the seller. Your real estate agent will coordinate these financial transactions to ensure a secure and efficient process.

Recording the Transfer and Taking Possession

The final step in closing the sale involves recording the transfer of ownership with the county recorder's office. This legalizes the change of ownership and ensures that the property's title is appropriately updated.

After the recording is complete, the buyer takes possession of the property. This transition is facilitated by your real estate agent, who ensures that all necessary documents and keys are handed over to the new owner.

Embracing Efficiency: Strategies for a Smooth Closing

To ensure an efficient closing process, clear and open communication is paramount. Regularly connect with your real estate agent and legal advisors to address any concerns or questions that arise. Be prepared to promptly provide any requested documentation and stay informed about the buyer's financing and title search progress.

It's also advisable to be flexible with your schedule, as the closing date might need to be adjusted due to unforeseen circumstances. Approach the closing process with a cooperative mindset, aiming to resolve any potential issues collaboratively to avoid unnecessary delays.

In conclusion, the closing process represents the final chapter of your real estate journey. By adhering to meticulous preparation, maintaining open lines of communication, and embracing a collaborative approach, you can efficiently navigate the intricacies of the closing process. The culmination of your efforts at the closing table marks the successful completion of a transformative endeavor—a journey that leads to the next phase of your life's adventure.

CHAPTER 20

The Path to Success: Implementing Your Home Selling Blueprint

As you arrive at the final chapter of this comprehensive guide, you stand ready to transform knowledge into action. The journey you've undertaken, traversing the pages of this book, has equipped you with insights, strategies, and a blueprint for navigating the intricate realm of selling your home. Now, let's consolidate these learnings and chart a clear path to success, guiding you toward implementing the home-selling blueprint you've cultivated.

1. Master Your Mindset: Embrace the Role of a Strategic Seller

Remember that your mindset shapes your experience. Approach the selling process with an open mind, ready to adapt, learn, and make informed decisions. Cultivate a positive outlook that not only uplifts your spirits but also resonates with the anticipated outcome you desire.

It's crucial to recognize the profound influence your mindset carries over every facet of this process. Your mindset is the compass that guides your actions, shapes your perception, and ultimately defines your experience. The selling process comprises many decisions, negotiations, and emotions, and your mindset orchestrates and sets the tone for this symphony. Embracing the role of a strategic seller involves adopting a multifaceted approach to your mindset:

Open-Mindedness: Approach the selling process with an open mind, unburdened by preconceived notions. Be willing to explore new strategies, consider different perspectives, and adapt to changing market dynamics. An open mind allows you to seize unexpected opportunities and navigate challenges with agility.

Lifelong Learning: Understand that selling your home is not just a transaction—it's a learning experience. Empower yourself with knowledge about market trends, negotiation techniques, and the legal aspects of real estate. A commitment to learning positions you as an informed and confident seller.

Informed Decision-Making: Base your decisions on well-researched analysis rather than impulsive reactions. Dive into available data, seek expert advice, and carefully assess the advantages and disadvantages before making substantial choices. A strategic seller approaches decision-making with careful consideration and purpose.

Positive Outlook: Cultivate a positive outlook that radiates through every interaction. A positive attitude not only uplifts your spirits but also resonates with potential buyers. Buyers are drawn to homes that exude positivity and warmth, making them more likely to envision a future within your property.

Resilience: Understand that the selling process may have its share of highs and lows. Embrace resilience as a core trait of a strategic seller. Challenges are growth opportunities, and setbacks are steppingstones to success. Approach obstacles with determination and a solution-oriented mindset.

By nurturing these aspects of your mindset, you're setting the stage for a transformative selling experience. As you navigate the intricacies of pricing, negotiations, and closing, your mindset will be your unwavering companion, guiding you with poise and purpose. Keep in mind you're not just selling a property; you're crafting a purposeful narrative that harmonizes with your objectives, captivates the interest of prospective buyers, and lays the foundation for a prosperous and gratifying transaction.

2. Prepare with Purpose: Setting the Stage for a Compelling Sale

Preparation is the cornerstone of a successful home sale. It involves recognizing that your home is not just a physical structure but a canvas on which potential buyers will project their dreams. Dedicate time and effort to prepare your property meticulously, focusing on decluttering and depersonalizing the space.

To achieve a well-organized and inviting environment, consider consulting professional organizers. They can provide valuable guidance on decluttering and streamlining your home, ensuring it appeals to a broad range of potential buyers.

Staging is a transformative process that goes beyond aesthetics. It involves arranging your home's layout, decor, and ambiance to ignite the imagination of potential buyers. By staging, you create an irresistible atmosphere that helps buyers visualize themselves living in your home. Staging not only enhances the visual appeal but also fosters an emotional connection that can lead to quicker and more favorable offers.

Ultimately, the goal of preparation is to maximize your home's visual allure. When done purposefully, preparation can significantly impact the first impression your home makes on potential buyers.

3. Understand Your Audience: Tailoring Your Message

Tailoring your marketing strategy is not a one-size-fits-all endeavor; it requires meticulous care and a deep understanding of your potential buyers. To effectively reach your target audience, consider the following:

Demographics: Begin by defining the demographic profile of your ideal buyer. Consider factors related to the type of community where your home is located, such as whether it's in a retirement neighborhood, an urban downtown area, or a suburban setting. Tailor your messaging to resonate with the characteristics that align with your property's location and features.

Preferences: Explore the lifestyle preferences that your potential buyers may seek in your home. Revisit in your mind the lifestyle preferences your neighborhood holds will allow you to showcase the aspects of your property that align with potential buyers' desires.

Aspirations: Beyond demographics and preferences, tap into the aspirations of your target audience. Craft your messaging to show how your home can be a stepping stone toward achieving their aspirations.

Multi-Channel Marketing: Leverage a blend of marketing techniques to ensure your property captures the ideal buyers' attention. Embrace digital platforms like social media and online listings to reach tech-savvy individuals.

Traditional Marketing: Don't underestimate the power of traditional marketing methods. Design eye-catching flyers and brochures that highlight the unique features of your property. Distribute these materials in local communities and at strategic locations.

Social Media: In the digital age, social media is a powerful tool for reaching a vast audience. Create engaging content that showcases the lifestyle your property offers. Utilize platforms like Facebook, Instagram, and Google to share high-quality images and videos, along with compelling descriptions.

Online Listings: Ensure your property is featured on popular real estate websites and listings. Include comprehensive details, professional photographs, and, if possible, virtual tours to provide potential buyers with an in-depth view of your home.

Email Campaigns: Craft targeted email campaigns to reach individuals who have expressed interest or are on your mailing list. Provide them with updates about your property, including any price changes or upcoming open houses.

By tailoring your message to your target audience's specific demographics, preferences, and aspirations and employing a multi-channel marketing approach, you'll significantly enhance your chances of attracting the ideal buyers for your property. Effective communication is vital to making a lasting impression and securing a successful sale. If you hire a real estate agent to help you navigate the sale, these are strategies and techniques your agent may employ for a successful sale.

4. Navigate Negotiations: Achieving Win-Win Outcomes

Embrace flexibility and open-mindedness during negotiations. Collaborate with your real estate agent to strategically respond to offers, concessions, and requests—endeavor to create a mutually beneficial transaction that satisfies both parties.

The ultimate goal of negotiation is to create a win-win situation. This means that both you, as the seller, and the buyer should walk away from the table feeling satisfied. This might involve compromises and creative solutions, such as adjusting the closing date or including certain appliances in the sale.

A successful negotiation isn't just about getting the highest price; it's about crafting a transaction that benefits both parties. This can foster goodwill and positive relationships, which are especially valuable if you're selling a home in a tight-knit community.

5. Grasp Financial Dynamics: Maximizing Returns

Maximizing returns in the real estate market begins with making well-informed investment decisions. This involves careful evaluation of potential upgrades or renovations and their expected return on investment (ROI). By identifying improvements that provide the highest ROI, such as kitchen remodels or curb appeal enhancements, you can effectively increase your property's perceived value. Wise investments not only attract more potential buyers but also lead to quicker sales and potentially higher offers.

Another crucial aspect of financial success in real estate is your pricing strategy. Collaborate closely with your real estate agent to gain valuable insights into local market conditions, enabling you to set the ideal price for your property. A well-considered price tag not only draws in more interested buyers but can also expedite the sales process and potentially result in more lucrative offers. Careful attention to your property's financial aspects, from investments to pricing, ensures you maximize your returns and create a more secure financial future.

6. Staying the Course: Avoiding Common Pitfalls

As you embark on your journey to implement your home selling blueprint, it's equally crucial to be aware of common pitfalls that can hinder your progress. Avoiding these missteps will help you stay on course and maximize your chances of a successful sale. Below are a few insights shared earlier on how to steer clear of common pitfalls.

Overlooking Property Condition: While you might be eager to sell, it's essential not to neglect property maintenance. Overlooking necessary repairs or presenting a poorly maintained property can deter potential buyers and lead to lower offers. Take the time to address maintenance issues to secure the best possible deal.

Neglecting Tenant Consideration: If your home is occupied by tenants, it's essential to involve them in the selling process. Failing to inform tenants of your intention to sell can lead to discomfort and reluctance to cooperate. Instead, communicate openly, consider their needs, and negotiate a plan that ensures a smooth transition for both parties.

Neglecting Legal Obligations: Selling a property involves legal obligations and paperwork. Neglecting these aspects or attempting to cut corners can result in legal disputes and complications. Consult with legal professionals to ensure that all necessary documentation is in order and that you're adhering to local regulations.

By being mindful of these common pitfalls and taking proactive steps to avoid them, you'll enhance your ability to execute your home selling blueprint smoothly and successfully. Remember, the journey to a successful sale is built on preparation, communication, and informed decision-making.

7. Seamless Closing: The Grand Finale

Navigating the closing process efficiently is paramount for a successful home sale. This stage involves collaborating closely with a team of professionals to address various legal formalities, title matters, necessary repairs, and the actual transfer of property ownership.

As you approach the closing date, it's crucial to make thorough preparations. This includes ensuring that all previously agreed-upon repairs and improvements are completed to the satisfaction of both parties. A final walkthrough is typically conducted to verify that the property is in the expected condition.

Throughout this process, it's essential to maintain open lines of communication with your real estate agent, attorney, and other involved professionals. They will guide you through the necessary paperwork, legal requirements, and financial transactions. By attending to every detail and collaborating effectively, you can confidently conclude the sale, knowing that you've successfully navigated every step of the home selling journey.

8. Chart Your Path to Success

Now, the path to implementing your home selling blueprint is clear:

Assess and Organize: Review your property, considering its unique features, location, and market trends. Organize all documentation related to your home and finances.

Consult with Experts: Engage with a trusted real estate agent who can provide personalized guidance based on your property and goals. Seek advice from financial advisors, legal experts, and professionals in the field.

Strategize and Price: Collaborate with your agent to strategically set the price, considering the local market, comparable properties, and your objectives.

Enhance and Stage: Implement the preparation strategies detailed in earlier chapters, from decluttering to enhancing curb appeal. If needed, stage your home to showcase its full potential.

Market and Negotiate: Employ traditional and digital marketing tactics to create a compelling listing. Collaborate with your agent to handle negotiations and navigate buyer offers.

Prepare for Closing: Work closely with your agent and legal advisors to ensure all paperwork is in order. Address any title issues, complete repairs, and get ready for the final walkthrough.

Celebrate the Sale: Once the transaction is finalized, take a moment to savor your success. This is not just the closing of a real estate deal; it's the culmination of a journey filled with careful planning, strategic decision-making, and hard work. It's a testament to your determination and the fulfillment of your goals.

As you celebrate, embrace the new chapter that awaits you. Whether it's moving into a new home, relocating to a different city, or embarking on a new life adventure, this is a time to look ahead with excitement and anticipation.

Consider marking this moment with a small gathering, a toast to your accomplishments, or simply taking a moment of reflection. It's a well-deserved opportunity to acknowledge your achievements and embrace the possibilities that lie ahead.

You can confidently implement your home selling blueprint by embracing each step of this path. Throughout this journey, remember that knowledge empowers action. As you take the steps outlined in this book, you're not just selling a property—you're on a transformational experience that shapes your financial future and paves the way for new horizons.

May your home selling experience be fulfilling, and may your endeavors lead to a successful and rewarding sale.

About the Author

Toi Holliday is a dedicated real estate professional with over two decades of experience in the client service industry. Her comprehensive background encompasses various facets of real estate, from investment and traditional sales to short-sale foreclosures, probate, trusts, land transactions, vacant properties, distressed, and tax-delinquent properties. This extensive experience equips her with a detailed understanding of the intricacies of real estate transactions.

Toi is the author of Maximizing Your Vacant Property, Home Selling Secrets Unveiled and several other educational resource guides offering vital insights for successfully navigating the real estate process. Through her written guidance, she empowers sellers and buyers to make informed decisions in their real estate journey.

Committed to excellence, Toi combines her passion for assisting people with her expertise to create a comprehensive approach to serving a diverse clientele.

As a Realtor® based in Los Angeles, California, Toi is active in her communities and holds memberships in various local and global associations. She enjoys spending time with her family and friends in her spare time, hiking, and traveling.

For more information about the author, visit:
www.ToiHolliday.com
CalDRE# 02018834

Scan Here

Home Selling Secrets Unveiled

Cover design by Bjou Brzee Creations.
Printed in the United States of America
First Printing: September 2023

www.ingramcontent.com/pod-product-compliance
Lightning Source LLC
Chambersburg PA
CBHW072309290526
45794CB00002B/582